A CONVERSATION BOOK 1
English in Everyday Life
Revised Third Edition

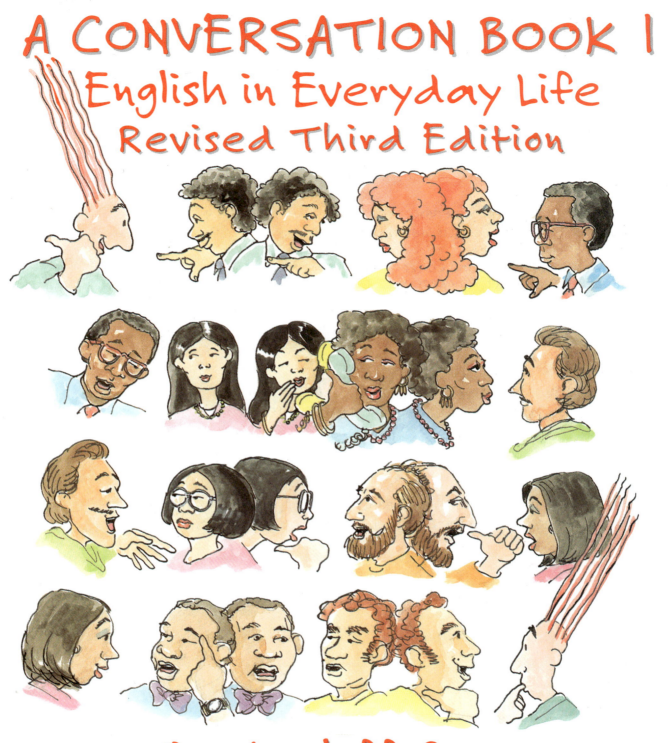

Tina Kasloff Carver
Sandra Douglas Fotinos

PRENTICE HALL REGENTS
A VIACOM COMPANY

Prentice Hall Regents
Upper Saddle River, New Jersey 07

Publisher: *Louisa B. Hellegers*
Development Editors: *Gino Mastascusa, Barbara Barysh*
Electronic Production Editors: *Christine Mann, Carey Davies*
                                  Michelle LoGerfo

Electronic Art Production Supervisor: *Ken Liao*
Electronic Publishing Specialist: *Steven Greydanus*
Art Director: *Merle Krumper*
Interior Design: *Noel Vreeland Carter*
Manufacturing Manager: *Ray Keating*

Illustrator: *Andrew Lange*

© 1998 by Prentice Hall Regents
Prentice-Hall, Inc.
A Simon & Schuster Company
Upper Saddle River, New Jersey 07458

Printed in the United States of America
10 9 8 7 6 5 4 3 2

0-13-792433-X

Prentice-Hall International (UK) Limited, *London*
Prentice-Hall of Australia Pty. Limited, *Sydney*
Prentice-Hall Canada Inc., *Toronto*
Prentice-Hall Hispanoamericana, S.A., *Mexico*
Prentice-Hall of India Private Limited, *New Delhi*
Prentice-Hall of Japan, Inc., *Tokyo*
Simon & Schuster Asia Pte. Ltd., *Singapore*
Editora Prentice-Hall do Brasil, Ltda., *Rio de Janeiro*

CONTENTS

UNIT 1: WELCOME TO CLASS   1

UNIT 2: EVERYDAY LIFE 13

UNIT 3: THE CALENDAR   25

UNIT 4: FOOD 41

UNIT 5: HOMES 61

UNIT 6: SHOPPING
81

UNIT 7: COMMUNITY   105

UNIT 8: WORK 127

UNIT 9: HEALTH 149

UNIT 10: LEISURE

FOREWORD

The Revised Third Edition of **A CONVERSATION BOOK 1** comes only three years after the Third Edition, in response to requests from many teachers for a split edition. Almost immediately after the Third Edition was published in 1994—featuring a picture dictionary format with a variety of student-centered activities—we started receiving requests for a split edition. Since the book contains so much material, some teachers wanted to spread **A CONVERSATION BOOK 1** lessons over two semesters; others simply wanted more options to choose from. Most also asked for sample conversations and a handy reference section of grammar for conversation.

If you are one of the many teachers who wrote or talked to us, this edition is our response to your requests. If you are not, we hope you will like the changes we have made here to give **A CONVERSATION BOOK** greater flexibility without sacrificing any of the spirit or the content of the original.

The Revised Third Edition is available as either a full edition or a split edition (1A and 1B). Both editions have Conversation Springboards and Grammar for Conversation sections in the Appendix, and the Conversation Springboards as well as the discrete vocabulary are also available on audiotape cassettes.

As with the Third Edition, a page-by-page Teacher's Edition, a separate, duplicatable Testing Program, and boxed, color transparencies are available to supplement the text.

The new edition remains true to the original concept of **A CONVERSATION BOOK**: that students acquire conversation skills best when their own experiences and interests are part of the conversation, and that student-centered, cross-cultural materials with extensive vocabulary and engaging illustrations focused on everyday life can help make the learning process a pleasure. We hope that **A CONVERSATION BOOK 1**, **REVISED THIRD EDITION** will help to make your conversation class a meaningful, enjoyable, and memorable learning experience for you and your students.

ACKNOWLEDGMENTS

No book is ever written in isolation. We could never begin to cite all the teachers we have spoken with, the programs we have been able to observe, and the authors who have influenced the writing of this book. They all have been part of our education and developing expertise as authors. We are indebted to them all, as well as to those teachers and students who have used the last two editions of the **CONVERSATION BOOK**.

The process of getting a book from first concept to press and out to the classroom involves many people. We were fortunate to have had dedicated, competent support during this time. For the Third Edition, which is the basis of the revised edition, our sincere appreciation goes to Nancy Baxer, our editor. Noël Vreeland Carter, our production editor, combined her remarkable skills in designing and editing with a great sensitivity to ESL and to the visual presentation, which has resulted in a masterfully produced book—both student-friendly and usable. Andrew Lange, our artist, embarked on this venture with an open mind and a wonderful spirit, and has combined his creative artwork with understanding and humor. The result is a whole new artistic pedagogy—a major focus of change in the third edition.

Also, thanks to Barbara Barysh, Andy Martin, and Gil Muller, as well as to H.T. Jennings, Karen Chiang, and Norman Harris, for their professional contributions and personal support. A word of thanks to our reviewers for their assistance in pointing the way to us and for their constructive, helpful, and supportive comments. Thanks to Ann Creighton, Edwina Hoffman, Laurie Ogilvie Lewis, Toni Hadi, Roni Lebauer, Barbara Wiggin, Greg Cossu, Kay Ferrell, and Kedre Murray.

The split editions are the result of a collaborative effort of many people. However, our sincere thanks and great appreciation must go first to Gino Mastascusa, who became our partner in every way. Gino's dedication, creativity, attention to detail, and unflagging long hours and hard work have further improved these texts. No words of thanks are really adequate. Kudos to you, Gino. Barbara Barysh, who helped in so many ways in the third edition, lent a superb editorial eye to this revision by catching so many inconsistencies and suggesting ways to make the materials more easily taught. Thanks also to Janet Johnston for her excellent support in the development of the text.

In a text such as this, production qualities are of utmost importance. The appeal to the student, the "look" as well as the accessibility, contribute to its pedagogy almost as much as the content itself. Christine Mann did a masterful production of the texts, further proving her excellence in her craft. Thanks to Carey Davies, for his additional technical support and extraordinary revisions of the maps.

Our sincere thanks to Louisa Hellegers, our publisher, who took the ideas of the field and helped mold them into reality. Because of Louisa, these texts have been published with the values and the timeliness they needed to serve the market.

Our appreciation goes to Ki Chul Kang, ELT manager in Korea, who for years, gathered information and suggestions from teachers in Asia, and helped mold for us this new revision. Also, Steven Golden, Nancy Baxer, Stephen Troth, Gunawan Hadi, Jerene Tan—thanks for your support both now and over the years.

Our thanks to Professor H. Douglas Brown, who guided us through the Learning Strategies and made great suggestions for our activities.

The list could go on and on—and fearful that we have omitted someone, we thank also Betty Azar, Tom Dare, Mike Bennett, Gordon Johnson, Susan Fesler, Rob Walters, and Maria Angione. Apologies to those we have missed and who also deserve credit!

Our own personal experiences as ESL teachers as well as foreign language learners underlie every page of **A CONVERSATION BOOK 1**. As learners, living and working in other countries, we were reminded daily that learning a new culture and a new language is very hard work! To the many people who have afforded us friendship when we were far from home, helped us deal with the complexity of everyday life in a new place, and patiently shared perceptions and languages with us, thank you. Without those experiences and without those people to guide us, **A CONVERSATION BOOK 1** would never have been written.

A Personal Word from Tina Carver

It is rare that an *editor* is afforded the opportunity to thank *authors*, but this time, the role reversal is appropriate. I have the good fortune to be associated with several people who professionally exhibit the highest level of excellence to which I aspire, and who, through the years, have also become very good friends. I will always value that friendship. So, to Betty Azar, Bill Bliss, Doug Brown, Robert Lado, and Steve Molinsky, thank you—so much of the improvement in this revision is the result of the many years of our professional conversations and work together.

A special note of appreciation goes to Sandra Fotinos, my master teacher of so many years ago, whose expert teaching and instincts towards students' needs have set an example to me throughout my career. Through all these years and experiences, both personal and professional, we have remained friends and colleagues.

I would like to express my appreciation to my three children, Jeffrey, Brian, and Daniel. They were all barely pre-schoolers when the first edition was published. Now college students, they watched over my shoulder as the third edition came to fruition. Their daily help and understanding—from reading the manuscript and offering suggestions to doing the cooking, laundry, shopping, and walking the dogs—made my work easier and, indeed, possible. My mother and father, Ruth and George Kasloff, influenced my early decision-making. My mother has continued to guide and to support me in all my endeavors. Finally, I would like to express my appreciation to Gene Podhurst for his cheerful and helpful contributions. He has read every page of the student text and the Teacher's Edition and the Testing Program over and over—and over— again. His excellent suggestions and insightful comments on the pedagogy and the execution of the ideas have added greatly to the new level of interest and the improvements made in this third edition.

A Personal Word from Sandra Fotinos-Riggs

I would like to thank my colleagues at Cochise College, Northern Essex Community College, and Harvard University for the many good years of stories and teaching techniques that we have shared, and for the constant, gentle reminder that what works once does not necessarily work again in another class or for another teacher.

For whatever I have really learned of living across cultures and languages through the delights and the hard times of everyday life, I want to say thank you to my Fotinos family-by-marriage, and especially to my mother-in-law, Kleopatra Fotinou, of Kallitsaina, Messinias, who has been for over thirty years, my Greek teacher and a loving, understanding friend.

Finally, thank you again to my children, Christina, Elizabeth, and Paul, who, like Tina's children, grew up with the **CONVERSATION BOOKS**, and whose cross-cultural life experiences are imbedded in so many of the conversations of the books. And, for the personal support without which this revision would have been impossible, thank you to Gene Riggs, my incredibly patient husband, and Tina Carver, for twenty-five years my co-author and friend.

New York/Arizona
July 1997

TO THE TEACHER

Our intention in writing **A CONVERSATION BOOK 1** was to provide a wide variety of vocabulary and student-centered learning activities for you to use within your own style and that of your beginning and low intermediate students.

Equally important is creating an atmosphere of shared learning in which students' differences are valued and their life experiences are appreciated. Learning a foreign language is perhaps the most threatening of all disciplines yet among the most rewarding. In the conversation class, students need to feel the class is a partnership—one between teacher and student as well as between student and student.

THE FIRST CLASS

The most important goal on the first day of class is to set a supportive, non-threatening learning environment. The room should be pleasant and welcoming; if possible, provide a way of relaxation for the students (who may be quite anxious), such as playing music when they arrive and/or offering coffee and tea and a snack. This will prove to be a worthwhile investment of time and thought.

- Provide name tags for all students (either just first names or both first and last). Wear one yourself.
- Spend time talking with students even before tackling the Welcome to Class! section. (Perhaps you don't even want to use the text during the first class; instead, have an informal, ice-breaking session. Use the *material* of the text but without the text itself.)
- Introduce yourself, speaking slowly. Ask, *"What's your name?"* If a student doesn't understand, use another student as a model, or ask *yourself* and answer it as a model. Try to scout any students who may know a little more and use them as models, too. Write the questions on the board to help students who may recognize written words but not be able to understand what you are saying. As the semester proceeds, both you and your students will learn to understand each other's speech. In the meantime, provide written reinforcement to reduce anxiety.

Suggestion

- Bring a large, lightweight ball to class.
- Have students stand in a circle. Participate in the first round.
- Hold the ball. Say your name and throw the ball to a student (Student 1) you are relatively sure will respond.
- Motion to Student 1 to repeat your name.
- Have Student 1 say his or her name and throw the ball to another student (Student 2) who says Student 1's name. Then as Student 2 throws the ball, he or she says his or her own name.
- Explain *throw* and *catch* by *doing* the actions.
- Repeat the game until all students have had a chance or two to give their own name.
- Do this activity as an entire class or in groups, depending on the size of the class.

This will be a gentle beginning into the more intricate movements of Total Physical Response (TPR) activities.

You will notice a "mascot" throughout the book. Sometimes he is sitting on the vocabulary boxes, sometimes he is integrated into the drawings. You and the class may want to *name* the mascot during the first session. This could be an enjoyable "Name Game." Ask the class to suggest names for him. List the names on the board. Then have the class vote on the names and give him the name the students select.

LEARNING STRATEGIES

The Learning Strategies box on the first page of every unit suggests ways to facilitate learning for the unit. This small section is designed to guide students to understand, appreciate, develop, and broaden their own learning styles. Discuss each strategy with the students as you begin the unit. Have students concentrate on the strategies throughout the unit and have them continue to practice the strategies from previous units. Add strategies as everyone in the class becomes aware of his or her unique learning style.

Read out loud the introduction (To the Student) from Professor H. Douglas Brown and discuss the advantages of understanding how each individual has his or her own way to learn most effectively.

VOCABULARY

Although the lessons in the full as well as the split editions of **A CONVERSATION BOOK 1** are designed for use either sequentially or in random order, the words are listed only once—the first time they appear on a text page. Keep this in mind if you are not using the book sequentially, from beginning to end. Every lesson has at least one vocabulary box. The list in the box is *not* exhaustive, but it does give the basic vocabulary for the lesson. Although words are not repeated in the subsequent boxes, the *items* are found repeatedly throughout the text in the illustrations. For example, in the full edition the word **shirt** appears first in the lesson on **Clothing and Colors** (Unit 1). The word does not appear in the vocabulary box in the **Men's Clothing Store** lesson (Unit 6), but a shirt appears in the *illustration* for that lesson. This device can serve as a review. Use the Alphabetical Word List in the Appendix to find the words and their original page references.

We have suggested several ways to present the vocabulary in the **Teacher's Edition**. Ultimately, the best methods depend upon your own style of teaching and the students' style of learning. You may want to discuss the illustration first, using the text or the transparency. This allows students to utilize what they already know and lets you assess the class' level of vocabulary proficiency. It also gives an immediate context for the vocabulary. Alternatively, you can simply point to each illustration and ask for the words. This way students associate the illustration with the English word. Combine methods for variety. Any method loses its effectiveness if used over and over again.

Every vocabulary box has lines for students to write vocabulary they contribute to the class discussion. These can be words students already know or words they want to learn (through a dictionary, other students, or you as the teacher-resource). Make these student-generated words part of the lesson, too.

Modeling the words for pronunciation is useful for students so they can *hear* how to *say* the word in English along with *seeing* the illustration and the *written* word. You can now use the Audio Program for practice in pronouncing the discrete words of each lesson, or model the words you see. Although sometimes it is difficult for you to hear all the pronunciations, choral repetition will give all students an opportunity to verbalize the words they are learning. Be sure students understand all the words. Sometimes native language translation is appropriate; that is your judgment call!

NOTE TAKING

Suggest that students buy a notebook. Have students divide the notebook into four sections: **Vocabulary, Activities, Journal, Community Information.** When new words are generated in the classroom from discussion or from activities, students should record the words and information in the **Vocabulary** section of their notebooks. Write new words on the board for students to record more easily. The **Activities** section should be used for any activities the students do in class or at home. The **Journal** section can be used for additional Journal writing.

The **Community Information** section should be a place to note valuable information about the students' communities. There are specific suggestions in the **Teacher's Edition** as to how and when to use the notebook.

CONVERSATION SPRINGBOARDS

Here are dialogs for teachers who hate dialogs! We have developed these springboards as conversation starters, to serve as models and inspirations for students to talk about their life experiences. They are not designed to be used for pattern practice! They are intentionally longer than traditional dialogs because they are meant for listening to and understanding real, whole conversations about everyday life in English. An accompanying Audio Program is available, which includes all of these Conversation Springboards.

Cassette icons [icon] on student-text pages signal where to use the audiotape. Each icon is footnoted with a cross-reference to the **Appendix** page with the corresponding Conversation Springboard.

There are five types of Conversation Springboards: *What's the process?, What's happening?, What happened?, What's next?,* and *What's your opinion?* Each type has a specific purpose.

- *What's the process?* Conversation Springboards are to be used *before* specified activities, and are intended to help students understand and talk about the purpose and process of the activity, as well as possible complications and their solutions.
- *What's happening?* Conversation Springboards tell a story, happening in the present. These dialogs are intended to help students listen to conversational narratives in present time, and to retell stories chronologically, using present and present progressive tenses.
- *What happened?* Conversation Springboards relate a story that happened in the past, and give students practice listening to past-time narratives and retelling the events in order, using past tenses.
- *What's next?* Conversation Springboards tell a story without an ending, or with a next step implied but not stated. They give students practice in drawing conclusions from indirect information, as well as opportunities to create their own endings in future time.
- *What's your opinion?* Conversation Springboards present a situation where preferences and opinions are expressed, and give students opportunities to agree or disagree with them, express their own opinions, and participate in a class discussion of a topic.

We suggest this method of using the Conversation Springboards and accompanying Audio Program:

1. Listen to the entire conversation once, with books either open or closed, depending on the class level and preference.

2. Listen again, breaking up the conversation by stopping the tape after every two lines. Check for understanding. Define any words that are unclear. Whenever possible, have students write down unclear words and try to guess the meaning from context.

3. Listen to the entire dialog again. (If you have listened with books closed until now, listen with books open this time.)

4. Follow up by having students either explain the process, situation, or problem, or tell the story of the conversation, depending on which type of Conversation Springboard you are using.

5. You may wish to have students read the conversations out loud themselves, depending on the class level and preference. If you do, go slowly! Remember that these are beginning students and long conversations!

GRAMMAR FOR CONVERSATION

The Grammar for Conversation section of the Appendix consists of conversation–based grammar charts and lists for each unit. The charts focus on basic grammar constructions and lists of formulaic expressions that students need to use extensively in each unit. The grammar emerges from the conversations and activities in the unit and the Conversation Springboards.

The conversations in this book are not grammar based. On the contrary, the practical needs of conversation in everyday life form the basis of the grammar included in the text. As a result, many grammar constructions appear very early in the book. They are intended to serve as springboards for understanding and using grammar in the context of everyday conversation, not for studying the grammar of English in a more conventional, systematic way. Each grammar element in a chart or list appears only once in the **Appendix**, although the same grammar element can occur throughout the book. Thus, students should be encouraged to refer to grammar charts from early units continually throughout the semester. You might want to teach and/or review a particular construction for an activity before or after the activity. However, the emphasis should be on conversation and communication, not grammatical accuracy.

In keeping with the **CONVERSATION BOOK** philosophy, the Conversation Springboards and Grammar for Conversation serve as beginnings—ways to get started listening and talking with the class, and ways to spark individual thinking and creativity. English may be a new language to your students, but that newness should not prevent them from using it creatively and having fun in the process of learning it. Most of all, have fun with these conversations!

CORRECTIONS

Use your own best judgment in handling corrections. Too much correction inhibits students' ability to think coherently and works contrary to practicing coherent and fluent conversation skills. On the other hand, aim to strike a balance, teaching syntax as well as pronunciation at opportune times. Take note of the errors students are making. It is usually not helpful to interrupt the flow of students' conversations, but correct errors at the appropriate time later in class, without referring to any specific students.

GROUPING

Pairing partners can be done in a variety of ways. The easiest way is to have students seated next to each other be partners. However, since an objective of the partner activities is for students to get to know one another, having a variety of partners is essential. Pairing students in different ways maintains students' attention, moves them around the room, and helps them to learn each other's names.

Suggestion:
- Count the students in the class; then divide them in half by left side/right side or front/back.
- Hand out slips of paper to one half of the students.
- Ask them to write their full names on the paper and fold the paper.
- Collect all the folded papers, then walk through the other half of the class. Have each student pick one folded paper.
- When all the papers are handed out, instruct the students with the papers to find their partners and sit down together.
- Depending on the class (and your own teaching style), you may prefer an open free-for-all with everyone walking around at once, calling out names; or a more structured pairing may be more appropriate in which one student at a time reads the name on his or her paper. The student named raises his or her hand, and the two then sit together.

These methods of pairing can be used again and again, dividing the class in different ways to assure that students have many different partners and get to know everyone in the class by name.

Partners should always ask each other for their names; there is a place in each **Partner Activity** for students to write their **Partner's Name**.

For some activities, larger groups of students are necessary. Again, grouping students can be done in a variety of ways.

Suggestion:

- Have students count off numbers (1–4, 1–5, 1–6, etc.), then join those who have that number.
- To practice vocabulary, you may replace numbers with items from the current vocabulary list—colors, fruits, vegetables, flowers, seasons, etc.
- List the group names on the board (for example, with colors, Red, Black, Yellow, Green, etc.), then assign each student a color and have students form groups according to their assigned color.

After students get to know each other, informal methods of pairing or grouping usually work best. Sometimes you can let students choose a partner or set up their own groups. For other activities, depending on the subject matter, you may want to deliberately mix gender, ages, language groups, occupations, or opinions. Try to avoid cliques sitting together. Remind students that the only way to develop conversational fluency in English is to practice *in English*.

PARTNER ACTIVITIES

Partner activities give students non-threatening, one-on-one opportunities to interact on a personal level. They are the only activities in which every student in the class has to do 50% of the talking and has to listen on a one-on-one basis. We have included four types of partner activities: **Games, Interviews, Journals,** and **Role Plays.**

Games

There are two types of partner games: **Memory Games** and **Mime Games.** Always do a "dry run" with the class to make sure that students understand the task.

Memory Games
What Do You Remember?

- Divide the class into pairs.
- Have the class look at the illustration. Show the transparency. Discuss how to remember the details of the illustration as they are looking at it (how many people, what are the colors, what season is it, what activities do you see, etc.).
- Then have the students close their texts and turn to the **Activities** section of their notebooks.
- Have the pairs work together, brainstorming everything they remember about the illustration. Have each pair make one list and number each item so that it will be easy to count how many items they listed.
- When students have finished, encourage several pairs to dictate the things they remember as you write them on the board. Or have one of the partners write the list on the board. Give several students the opportunity to do this.
- Open the texts or show the transparency. Look at the illustration together.
- Draw a line under the last item listed and have students dictate additional items as you write them on the board.
- Point out new vocabulary for students to add to the **Vocabulary** section of their notebooks.

Same or Different?

- Divide the class into pairs.
- Have students study the illustrations they are going to compare. Show the transparency.
- Instruct the pairs to make one list of similarities and differences in the illustrations.
- Remind students to number each item so it will be easy to count how many items they listed.
- While students are working, write two horizontal headings: SAME and DIFFERENT.
- When students have finished their lists, have several pairs dictate their lists as you write the items on the board.
- Open the texts or show the transparency. Look at the illustrations together.
- Draw a line under the last item listed. Have students dictate additional items as you write them on the board.
- Point out new vocabulary for students to add to the **Vocabulary** section of their notebooks.

Vocabulary Challenges

- Divide the class into pairs.
- Books must be closed. "Challenge" pairs of students to make a list of as many vocabulary words and phrases as they remember from the lesson. Remind them to number the words as they write. Give them a time limit for completing the list.
- When the time is up, ask how many words and phrases each pair had.
- Have a pair read their entire list or copy it on the board. Star ★ the words that are *not* from the lesson. Have the class check off the words they have on their lists.
- Have another pair read *only* the words they have that *aren't* on the board. List the new words on the board. Double-star ★★ the new words.
- Have the class check off the words they have that are on the board.
- Have another pair read *new* words from their list. List the new words on the board. Triple-star ★★★ the new words. Have the class check off any words they have on their lists.
- Ask which pair has other new words. Add the words to the list.
- Ask which pair had the most new words. They "win" the challenge!

Mime Games

Sometimes students are asked to act out words or actions with a partner. Demonstrate the activity for the students first so they understand what to do. As the class is doing the activity, circulate; help as needed.

Interviews

It is important, especially during the first days of class, for the students to understand how to conduct these interviews. Your role is to model pronunciation, facilitate understanding of vocabulary and questions, and provide possible answers. For modeling, use a student who will catch on quickly; be careful not to use the same student all the time. Or, if it is more appropriate, model both roles yourself. Write the question and answer on the board so that students can *see* the questions and answers as well as *hear* them.

- Practice the interview questions with the students. Be sure they understand the questions and the vocabulary. Supply any additional words needed.
- Divide the class into pairs.
- Have students interview their partners. Circulate; help as needed.
- After partners conduct their interviews, have several pairs present their interviews to the class. Either have them present all questions or have different pairs present one question each. Alternatively, have them share what they have learned with another pair of students.

- Write new vocabulary generated from the interviews on the board. Have students copy the new words in the **Vocabulary** section of their notebooks.
- Use the students' responses to the interviews for further discussions which may be of interest to the class.

Journals

The journal entries give students a chance to use the vocabulary and phrases they have learned in writing reinforcement activities. Journals should be done as an interactive activity.

- Discuss the topic with the students before they begin to write.
- Model and practice the questions provided at the top of the page. Add your own questions, if appropriate.
- Divide the class into pairs.
- Have partners ask each other the questions. Circulate; help as needed.
- Have students do their individual journal writing in class or at home.
- Have students proofread their journals.
- Instruct partners to read their journals to each other; encourage them to ask questions and make comments.
- If there is time, have several students read their journals to the class.
- Alternatively, read several journals to the class and have students guess who wrote them.
- Have one or two students put their journal entries on the board. Write the skeleton paragraph as it appears in the text. Either you or the student can fill in the blanks. Have students read what they wrote on the board, or you can read it as a model. Discuss new vocabulary and new ideas.
- Take advantage of any additional topics or information that may emerge to continue conversations and exchanges of information.
- Students can keep more journal pages in the **Journal** section of their notebooks. Provide guidance for the topics and do light corrections. The object of journal pages is for students to have practice writing fluently in English and expressing their thoughts and emotions. Too much correction will inhibit this goal.

Role Plays

Before students do role-playing for the first time, do a sample role play using yourself and another student. This will provide a model for students when they are working independently.
- Divide the class into pairs.
- List the vocabulary needed on the board. Leave the vocabulary on the board as a reference for students when they are working with their partners.
- Students should write the conversation and practice reading their "scripts" with the "read and look up" technique. (*Have the students scan the line and remember it as well as they can; then have them look at the other person and SAY the line without READING it—even beginners can perfect this technique. The appropriate eye contact and body language required in English enhances this technique.*)
- Have several pairs present their role plays—with simple props, if appropriate.
- Encourage the pairs to come to the front of the room or sit in the middle of the circle rather than remain at their desks.
- For classes with shy students, an alternative to a traditional role play is a puppet show. Make hand puppets from small paper bags. Cover a table with a sheet for a stage. This activity can be simple or elaborate.

GROUP ACTIVITIES

Group activities give students a feeling of belonging and a feeling of being a part of the group's success. These activities allow students to get to know one another and to cooperate within the framework of different tasks. Many of the activities are cooperative; they require each member of the group to contribute something. While the groups are working, you can move from group to group as a facilitator to be sure students understand their task. After the groups complete the activity, have them report back to the class as a whole so that a summation and conclusions can be drawn. We have included seven types of group activities: **Conversation Squares, Discussions, Gossip Games, Problem Posing/Problem Solving, Surveys, Vocabulary Challenges,** and **What's the Story?**

Conversation Squares

- Have the students help you create the question they will need to ask for each square.
- Write the questions on the board.
- Construct boxes on the board similar to the ones in the text.
- Choose two students. Use yourself as the third member of the group.
- Put the three names on the top of the boxes as indicated in the text.
- Ask and answer the questions for your box; write in your responses.
- Ask your "partners" the questions. Write in their responses.
- Then ask the class the questions for more practice.
- Have groups of three do the activity.
- When all students have finished, ask different groups single questions from the conversation squares. Put new vocabulary on the board for students to write in the **Vocabulary** section of their notebooks.

Discussions

These activities consist of guided questions. Each group should appoint a *leader* to ask the questions and a *recorder* to record the answers. That way, when called upon to recite, the answers are written down and students can feel confident in their replies. Real learning in these activities goes on within the group's dynamic. Reporting back is a way to summarize. Students shouldn't feel intimidated by the reporting back part of the activity. Writing answers usually eliminates this anxiety.

During the "reporting back" stage, note new vocabulary, write it on the board, and have students write the new words in the **Vocabulary** section of their notebooks.

Gossip!

This is a variation of the "Gossip" or "Telephone" game. It has two objectives: to practice new vocabulary in context without visual cues and to demonstrate how information is lost in the process of retelling. A *secret* for each game is included in the **Appendix.**

- Divide the class into large groups, or do this activity with the whole class, if your class is small.
- Use the illustration on the text's cover to explain the game. Start on the top left with the mascot. End on the bottom right with the mascot.
- Have the *leader* from each group read the *secret* silently several times. All other students should have their books closed.
- Be sure to explain the words "whisper" and "secret." Have the *leaders* close their books and quietly whisper the *secret* to the student next to them. Those students quietly whisper it to the next, and so on.
- When all students have heard the *secret,* have the last student of each group report the information to the class, either orally or in written form on the board.
- Have everyone read the *secret* together to see what information was lost and changed.

Problem Posing/Problem Solving

- Divide the class into small groups.
- Do a practice Problem Posing/Problem Solving example with the class as a whole.

- Have each group choose a *recorder* and a *leader*. Each student should participate in some way.
- Before students begin, be sure that they understand the goal of the activity and that they have adequate vocabulary and grammar to do the work.
- Have students think about what is happening in the illustration and formulate a question about it (pose the problem). Remind the *leader* to ask the questions.
- Then have them think through (analyze) the problem and make a group decision as to what to do (solve the problem). This will take thought, negotiation, resolution, and consensus.
- To summarize, have each *recorder* report back to the class.
- Draw class conclusions, even if there is diversity of opinion and no real resolution.

Surveys

This activity gives students the opportunity to express their own opinions and preferences, and check their accuracy in listening and recording answers.
- Model the questions; have students repeat; check pronunciation.
- Be sure students understand all the vocabulary and the objective of the activity before the activity begins.
- Have students check off their own answers in the appropriate column.
- Divide the class into groups of seven to ten. If your class is small, do the activity with the whole class.
- Encourage the students to get up and walk around while asking questions. Remind them that each student should ask everyone in the group all the questions and check the appropriate column for every answer.
- Set a time limit. Tell students to sit down when they finish and count their results. Remind them to include their own answers in the count.
- Have students report their results to their group. If other members of the group have different numbers, have them figure out who is right.
- While groups are working, copy the chart on the board.
- When groups are sure of their numbers, have them report their results. Fill in the columns on the board and have students draw conclusions about the class.
- Point out new words and have students write them in the **Vocabulary** section of their notebooks.

Vocabulary Challenges

This activity is similar to the **Vocabulary Challenges** as described in the **Memory Games** section of **PARTNER ACTIVITIES**.

What's the Story?

The goal of this activity is to have students look at an illustration (which tells a story), then use their imaginations and the vocabulary they know to create their own story. These activities are cooperative learning activities. Each student should contribute one, two, or three lines. The story should be complete and make sense.
- Divide the class into groups.
- Have each group select a *recorder* to write everyone's lines.
- Encourage students to help each other. Be sure that even the shy students participate by contributing their lines.
- After the stories are written, all groups should listen to their *recorder* read the story. They should all make changes and corrections and "edit" the story before the rest of the class hears it. Have another student (*not* the *recorder*) read the story, or have each student read or recite his or her lines, or part of the narrative.
- Have the class decide which was the best, the most exciting, the saddest, the funniest, etc.

CLASS ACTIVITIES

Class activities provide opportunities for lots of input; this is the advantage of a large class. Many opinions and answers make the class more interesting and exciting. However, if your class functions better in smaller groups, these activities can work as Group Activities also. We have included seven types of class activities: **Community Activities, Cross-Cultural Exchanges, Discussions, Find Someone Who, Strip Stories, Total Physical Response (TPR) Activities,** and **Vocabulary Challenges.**

Community Activities

These activities give the class the opportunity to venture into the community and explore, as well as to discover community resources (for example, the telephone book) in the classroom itself. Students can be sent out individually, in groups, or with partners to gather information requested.

- Review the task before students are asked to do the work independently. Be sure students know the vocabulary and are clear about what they are to do.
- To help prepare students, role-play expected scenarios and outcomes. This may avoid pitfalls and panic!
- If possible, accompany the class the first time out. This will give them confidence.
- After the students do the assignment, review it in class.
- Discuss not only the task but what happened—what surprises they had, what reactions they had, how they felt, etc.
- Have students keep important community information in the **Community** section of their notebooks.

Cross-Cultural Exchanges

These activities give the class the opportunity to talk about cultural differences in general as well as about U.S./Canadian cultures. Students should be encouraged to voice their opinions and confusions about cultures they associate with the English language. Opportunities and interest in this activity will vary with your classes. Wherever possible, compare three or more cultures rather than just two to avoid potential "either/or" interpretations of differences. Encourage inter-cultural openness and awareness without judgment.

Discussion

Ask the guided questions and choose different students to answer each question. This provides a model for the students. As an alternative approach, you can ask the first question and choose a student to answer. Then have that student ask the second question and choose a student to answer. Continue the pattern. Correct only large errors that impede understanding.

To help structure discussions and teach note-taking skills, write a brief heading for each question on the board. Encourage students to do the same in the **Activities** section of their notebooks. List information you gather from the discussions under each heading. Then review your notes and ask the students to review theirs. Draw conclusions together from the notes at the end of the discussion.

Find Someone Who

This activity is similar to the **Survey** activity, except in this activity, students are searching for "Yes" answers.
- Review the vocabulary and create the Yes/No questions with the class before they start the activity. Write the questions on the board.
- Give students the grammar constructions in chunks. Review appropriate grammar from the **Appendix.**

- Have the class ask the questions by circulating around the class. If the class is very large, break the class into groups of 10–15 and have students do the activity within their group.
- When students have completed their work, have them sit in their seats.
- Review the questions and answers. There should be interesting "springboards of conversation" that come from the individual answers.

Strip Stories

This visual presentation of little stories gives students the opportunity to discuss the action in the frames and then to write their own captions.
- Have students look at the illustrations and discuss them together.
- Write vocabulary words on the board.
- Ask for suggestions for captions and/or bubbles.
- Write different suggestions on the board. Have students decide which one is best and why.
- Have students write captions in their texts.
- Alternatively, have students create captions individually, in groups, or with partners.

Total Physical Response (TPR) Activities

The first Total Physical Response (TPR) activity has illustrations for each of the steps. (See page 5 of the full edition.) After that, only the *instructions* for TPR activities appear in the text.
- Prepare students by giving out slips of paper that they will write something on—an instruction, a favorite month, a favorite food, etc.
- Always model the action before asking students to do it. The object of this activity is for students to associate the action with the words for it. Use exaggerated movements.
- After you demonstrate the action, have the class repeat that action.
- To review, have a student read the action and have the class follow the instruction.
- As a written review, dictate the action and have students write the dictation in the **Activities** section of their notebooks.

Vocabulary Challenges

This activity is similar to the **Vocabulary Challenges** as described in the **Memory Games** section of **PARTNER ACTIVITIES**.

INDIVIDUAL ACTIVITIES

These activities are designed for students to have the opportunity to share their individual perceptions, knowledge, and experiences with the whole class. There are three types of individual activities: **Draw**, **Speeches**, and **Tell the Class**.

Draw

Students don't have to be artists—nor do you—to do this. A rendition of what is called for is good enough for students to be able to talk about the drawing.
- Give students enough time to complete their drawing.
- Circulate; help as needed, but also scout students who will be able to share a useful drawing—either on the board, as a transparency, or with photocopies.
- Use your own artwork—the "worse" it is, sometimes, the better. Students are less reluctant to share theirs if yours *isn't* "good"!
- Have students talk about what they drew. Be sure to note new vocabulary words.

Speeches

Students get practice in simple speech writing and recitation with these activities. Give students ample time to prepare. Make the activity *very* structured and help correct as much as you can. Visual aids can help relieve anxiety. Allow students to have note cards, but not to read their speech. Sometimes it is helpful for students to practice with a partner or a small group before addressing the class. There are **Speech** and **Audience Evaluation Forms** in the **Appendix**.

Tell the Class

These activities give students the opportunity to be in front of the class and speak without much preparation. With some notes, a little confidence, and a supportive environment, their anxiety levels will be lowered.

TEACHER'S EDITION

The **Teacher's Edition**, interleaved with actual student-text pages, provides the teacher a convenient teaching tool. The format is easy to follow: **Warm Up** activities for each lesson precede the step-by-step suggestions for all **In the Text** activities. Objectives are clearly stated for each lesson. In addition, there is a wide variety of **Expansion** activities for each lesson. The **To the Teacher** section gives an overview of all activities and objectives.

TESTING PROGRAM

This program includes both conversation and vocabulary tests for each unit. Suggestions for administration with large and small classes are included. Permission to photocopy the tests is granted.

TRANSPARENCIES

A boxed set of **Color Transparencies** is available. These transparencies include *all* the illustrations from the picture dictionary pages as well as other illustrations which lend themselves to class discussions and activities. The transparencies can facilitate the introduction of the vocabulary lesson by allowing students to close their books and look up, rather than being engrossed in words and page turning. The transparencies focus students' attention and enable teachers to point out details more easily. The transparencies can also be used for class activities, for vocabulary review, and as an alternative testing instrument.

TO THE STUDENT

In **A CONVERSATION BOOK 1**, your teacher will help you to learn English by using it in conversations with English speakers. Your work in the classroom is very important. It will help you to practice English, to speak more clearly and fluently, and to listen to others carefully and understand what they are saying. But it is also very important for you to practice English *outside* of the classroom.

To help you to be a better learner of English, I have ten "rules" for successful language learning that I encourage you to follow. These rules suggest ways to help you become a successful learner. If you can follow this advice, you too will learn English more successfully. Here are the ten rules:

1. Don't be afraid!

Sometimes we are afraid to speak a foreign language because we think we are going to make terrible mistakes and people will laugh at us. Well, the best learners of foreign languages try not to be afraid. They make a "game" of learning. They are not anxious about making mistakes. And they sometimes share their fears with friends. You can do that, too, and you will then feel better about yourself.

2. Dive in!

Try to speak out! Try to say things in English! The best way to learn English is to speak it yourself. Don't worry about perfect pronunciation or grammar; other people usually will not criticize you.

3. Believe in yourself.

You have lots of strengths. You have already learned some English. You must believe that you *can* do it! Compliment your fellow learners on their efforts. Then maybe they will return the favor!

4. Develop motivation.

Why are you learning English? Make a list of your reasons for studying English. Those reasons can be your individual goals for this course. If you have your own reasons for learning English, you will have better success.

5. Cooperate with your classmates.

You are learning language in order to communicate with other people. So, practice with other people and you will be more successful. Create your own conversation group outside of class. Try out new ways to communicate in those groups. And, in class, remember your classmates are your "team" members, not your opponents.

6. Get the "big" picture!

Sometimes learners look too closely at all the details of language (words, pronunciation, grammar, usage). It's OK to pay attention to those details, but it is also important to understand general meanings (the "big" picture). Maybe you don't know all the right words or grammar, but you can say things, anyway. See movies in English. Read books and magazines for pleasure.

7. Don't worry if you're confused.

Learning English is a big task! Sometimes you will feel confused about all the things you have to learn in a foreign language. Try not to worry about everything all at once. Don't try to learn *all* the rules right now. Ask your teacher questions about English. And try to learn a little every day.

8. Trust your "hunches."

Sometimes people think they should analyze everything in their new language (grammar rules, word definitions). The best learners do some analyzing, but they follow their "hunches" (their best guesses, their intuitions) about the new language. If they have an intuition that something sounds right, they will try it. So, the next time you "feel" that something is right, say it. You'll probably be right, and, if you aren't, someone will give you some feedback.

9. Make your mistakes work FOR you.

A mistake is not always "bad." We all make mistakes learning anything new. Successful learners don't worry about mistakes; they learn from them. They take note of their errors and try to correct them the next time. Some things you can do:

- Make a list of your most common mistakes.
- Select grammar points to watch for.
- Tape-record yourself and listen for errors.

10. Set your own goals.

Teachers usually set goals (assignments, homework, classwork) for you. But *you* need to set your own goals, too. You can do that by doing the following:

- Set aside a certain number of hours a week for extra study.
- Learn a certain number of words a day/week.
- Read a certain number of extra pages a day/week.

Take charge of your own learning!

Try to follow at least some of these rules for successful language learning as you work with **A CONVERSATION BOOK 1**. I am sure that you will be a more efficient learner of English, and you will feel proud of your accomplishments. Good luck!

H. Douglas Brown, Ph.D.
American Language Institute
San Francisco State University
San Francisco, CA
May 1997

A CONVERSATION BOOK 1
English in Everyday Life
Revised Third Edition

WELCOME TO CLASS

LEARNING STRATEGIES

➤ Introduce yourself to your classmates. Learn their names and your teacher's name. Write them down. After class, introduce yourself to other speakers and learners of English.

➤ Start a notebook. Divide it into sections:
Vocabulary
Activities
Journal
Community Information

WELCOME TO CLASS!

Draw

Draw a picture of yourself.

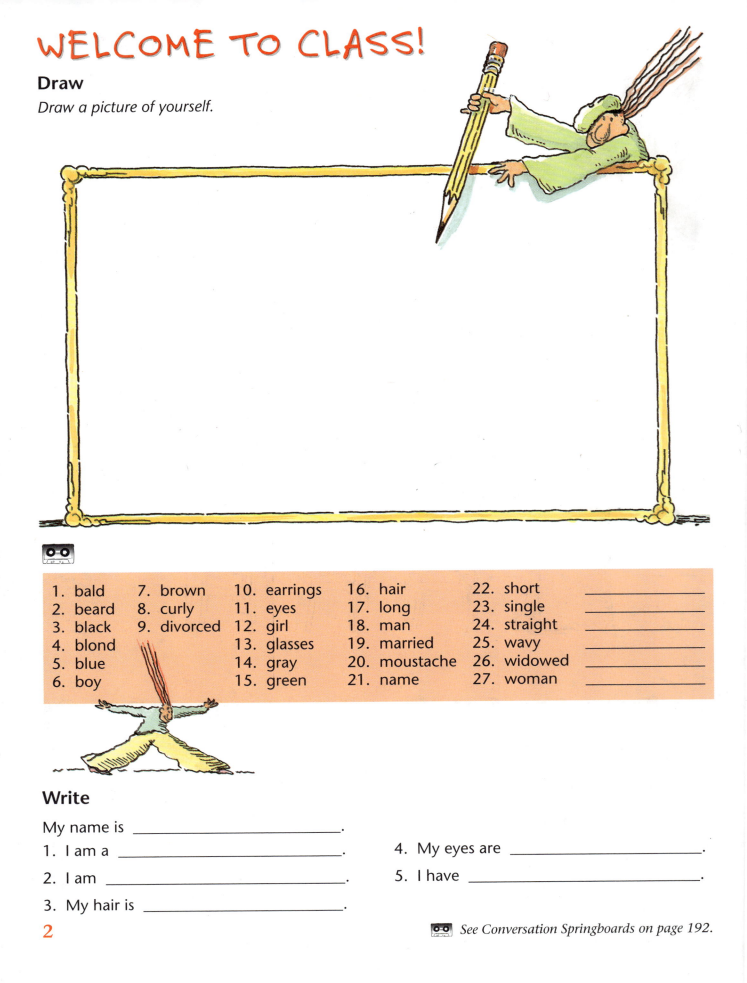

1. bald	7. brown	10. earrings	16. hair	22. short	_____
2. beard	8. curly	11. eyes	17. long	23. single	_____
3. black	9. divorced	12. girl	18. man	24. straight	_____
4. blond		13. glasses	19. married	25. wavy	_____
5. blue		14. gray	20. moustache	26. widowed	_____
6. boy		15. green	21. name	27. woman	_____

Write

My name is _____.

1. I am a _____.

2. I am _____.

3. My hair is _____.

4. My eyes are _____.

5. I have _____.

2   *See Conversation Springboards on page 192.*

Tell the Class*

Write your first name and your last name on the board. • *Tell the class your name.* • *Show your picture to the class.* • *Describe your picture.*

Partner Activity   Partner's Name _____

Introduce yourself to your partner. • *Practice all these ways.*

     A: My name is _____. What's your name? *(or)*
         Hello. I'm _____. What's your name? *(or)*
         Hi. I'm _____. What is your name?

     B: Nice to meet you. My name is _____. *(or)*
         I'm _____. I'm pleased to meet you.

Introduce your partner to the class.

         I'd like you to meet _____. *(or)*
         This is _____.

Group Activity

Work in groups of three or four. • *Write a name tag for yourself.* • *Pronounce the names of each student in your group.* • *Introduce yourself to the others in the group.*

COUNTRIES

1. Africa
2. Asia
3. Atlantic Ocean
4. Central America
5. city
6. continent
7. Europe
8. island
9. language
10. map
11. North America
12. Pacific Ocean
13. place
14. South America
15. world
_____
_____
_____
_____
_____

Class Activity

Find your country on the map. • *Circle the places on the map where all your classmates are from.* • *Draw a big star where you are now.*

Partner Interview*

Partner's Name _____

Practice these questions with your teacher. • *Then ask your partner.*

1. What is your name?
2. What country are you from?
3. What city are you from?

4. What continent are you from?
5. Where do you live now?
6. What languages do you speak?

Tell the Class

Tell the class about your partner.

See Conversation Springboards on page 192.

4

* See Appendix page 245 for Nations/Nationalities.

Class Game*: "Where do you want to visit?"

1. Think.

2. Write.

3. Fold.

4. Make a pile.

5. Open one. Read it to the class.

6. Guess who wrote it.

Tell the Class

Tell the class about the place you want to visit.

* See <u>Appendix</u> pages 240-244 for Maps.

NUMBERS

count			
0 zero	9 nine	18 eighteen	27 twenty-seven
1 one	10 ten	19 nineteen	28 twenty-eight
2 two	11 eleven	20 twenty	29 twenty-nine
3 three	12 twelve	21 twenty-one	30 thirty
4 four	13 thirteen	22 twenty-two	40 forty
5 five	14 fourteen	23 twenty-three	50 fifty
6 six	15 fifteen	24 twenty-four	60 sixty
7 seven	16 sixteen	25 twenty-five	70 seventy
	8 eight	17 seventeen	26 twenty-six

80 eighty
90 ninety
100 one hundred
_____
_____

Class Survey

Count the men and women in your class. • Write the correct number and word for each question. • What did you find?

	MEN	WOMEN
1. How many are there?	_____	_____
2. How many have ?	_____	_____
3. How many are ?	_____	_____
4. How many have blue ?	_____	_____
5. How many have ?	_____	_____
6. How many have ?	_____	_____
7. How many have a ?	_____	_____
TOTALS	_____	_____

Group Activity

Work in groups of four. • Write the names of all the students in your group. • Write what you remember about each student. • Compare notes with your group. • Read your group's list to the class.

6

See Conversation Springboards on page 192.

JOURNAL

Partner Interview

Practice these questions with your teacher. •
Then ask your partner.

Partner's Name _____

1. What's today's date?
2. How many students are in our class?
3. What is your name?
4. What color is your hair?
5. What color are your eyes?
6. Are you married or single?
7. Where are you from?
8. What language do you speak?

Write

Write about your partner.

Journal

_____
(1)

I am in my English class. There are _____ students
(2)

in my class today. My partner's name is _____.
(3)

She/He has _____ hair and _____ eyes.
(4)   (5)

My partner is _____. She/He is from _____ and
(6)   (7)

speaks _____.
(8)

Tell the Class

Read your journal to the class. • *Tell the class about your partner.*

 See Conversation Springboards on page 192.

CLOTHING AND COLORS

1. barrette	7. dress	13. purple	19. skirt	25. T-shirt
2. belt	8. gold	14. raincoat	20. sports coat	26. white
3. blouse	9. handkerchief	15. red	21. suit	27. yellow
4. button	10. jacket	16. scarf	22. sweater	28. zipper
5. coat	11. pink	17. shirt	23. sweatshirt	_____
6. collar	12. pocket	18. silver	24. tie	_____

Partner Game: *"What do you remember?"*   Partner's Name _____

Look at your partner's clothing. • Sit back to back. • Make a list of what your partner is wearing. • Read your list to your partner. • Don't look at your partner. • Correct your list with your partner.

Class Activity

List on the board the different colors the students are wearing. • How many men are wearing each color? • How many women are wearing each color? • What is the class' favorite color?

See Conversation Springboards on page 192.

PAIRS OF CLOTHING

1. boots
2. boxer shorts
3. gloves
4. jeans
5. jockey shorts
6. mittens
7. new

8. old
9. pajamas
10. panties
11. pants (slacks)
12. pantyhose
13. sandals
14. shoes

15. shorts
16. slippers
17. sneakers
18. socks
19. stockings
20. sunglasses

_____
_____
_____
_____
_____
_____
_____

Group Game: *"True or false?"*

Work in groups of four. • *Write three true statements about your clothes.* • *Write one false statement.* • *Read your statements to your group.* • *Who can guess the false statement?*

Group Game: *"What am I wearing?"*

Describe the clothing of a student in another group. • *Who can guess that student's name?*

See Conversation Springboards on pages 192 and 193.

FAMILY

1. grandmother }
2. grandfather } grandparents

3. mother }
4. father } parents

5. sister-in-law
6. brother-in-law
7. mother-in-law } in-laws
8. father-in-law

9. daughter }
10. son } children

11. dog }
12. cat } pets

13. adult
14. child

15. wife
16. husband

17. sister
18. brother } siblings

19. aunt
20. uncle
21. niece
22. nephew

23. single parent
24. cousin

See Conversation Springboards on page 193.

Tell the Class

Can you add more words to the list? • Tell the class about a favorite person in your family.

1. favorite	5. nice	9. short	13. wise
2. funny	6. old	10. sympathetic	14. young
3. heavy	7. photo	11. tall	
4. helpful	8. portrait	12. thin	

Partner Interview

Practice these questions with your teacher. • Then ask your partner.

Partner's Name _____

1. Is your family big or small?
2. How many people are in your family?
3. How many brothers and sisters do you have?
4. Are they older or younger?
5. Do you have children?
6. Do you have a pet?

Draw

Work in groups of four or five. • Draw a family portrait or a family tree. • Tell your group about your family.

Tell the Class

Bring in photos of your family. • Show your photos to the class. • Explain who everyone is.

See Conversation Springboards on page 193.

11

REVIEW

Partner Interview

Partner's Name _____

Ask your partner.

1. What is your name?
2. What color are your eyes?
3. What color is your hair?
4. Are you tall or short?
5. Do you wear glasses?
6. Are you married?
7. How many sisters do you have?
8. How many brothers do you have?
9. Where are you from?
10. What language do you speak?

Find Someone Who

Review the vocabulary with your teacher. • *Fill in the name of someone who . . .*

1. _____ speaks three languages.
2. _____ has three names.
3. _____ is from a small family.
4. _____ is wearing jeans.
5. _____ is from a big city.
6. _____ wants to visit Disney World.

EVERYDAY LIFE

LEARNING STRATEGIES

➤ Make vocabulary cards for new words. Study the cards every day. Memorize five new words every day.

➤ Talk in English with a classmate on your break every day.

THE CLASSROOM

1. board	8. door	15. pen	22. wall
2. book	9. doorknob	16. pencil	23. wastebasket
3. ceiling	10. eraser	17. point	24. window
4. chair	11. floor	18. raise your hand	_____
5. chalk	12. globe	19. student	_____
6. clock	13. notebook	20. table	_____
7. desk	14. paper	21. teacher	_____

14

See Conversation Springboards on page 193.

Draw

Draw a picture of your classroom. • *Include everything.* • *Work fast!* • *Compare pictures with other students.* • *Who had the most complete picture?*

Group Game: *"What is it?"*

Work in groups of six. • *Choose a leader.*

    Leader: *Think about something in the classroom. Don't say it!*
    Group: *Ask the leader YES/NO questions.*
    Leader: *Answer "Yes" or "No."*
    Group: *Try to guess what it is. Whoever guesses is the new leader.*

TAKING A BREAK

1. argue	7. go out	13. sit	19. think	_____
2. come in	8. laugh	14. sleep	20. walk	_____
3. cry	9. listen	15. smile	21. wave	_____
4. draw	10. look	16. speak	22. worry	_____
5. erase	11. read	17. stand	23. write	_____
6. frown	12. shake hands	18. talk	24. yawn	_____

See Conversation Springboards on page 193.

Class Game: *"What am I doing?"*

Think. • *Write an* <u>activity</u>. • *Fold your paper.* • *Make a pile of papers.* • *Open one.* • *Follow the* <u>instruction</u>. • *Ask "What am I doing?"* • *Have the class guess the activity.*

Partner Game: *"How are you today?"*   Partner's Name _____

Decide how they are today. • *Write in the bubbles.* • *Fill in your own.*

1. angry	4. hot	7. sick	_____
2. cold	5. hungry	8. thirsty	_____
3. happy	6. nervous	9. tired	_____

Group Vocabulary Challenge

Work in groups of four. • *What do you do on a break?* • *Make a list with your group.* • *Read your group's list to the class.* • *With the class, make a list of the new words on the board.* • *Copy the new words into your notebook.*

See Conversation Springboards on page 193.   **17**

TIME

1. afternoon
2. alarm clock
3. a.m.
4. clock radio
5. digital clock
6. early
7. eat breakfast
8. eat dinner
9. eat lunch
10. evening
11. get up
12. go to bed
13. go to class
14. hour
15. late
16. midnight
17. minute
18. morning
19. night
20. noon
21. on time
22. p.m.
23. second
24. study
25. wake up
26. watch

Class Discussion

What time is it in the pictures? • *What is the student doing?* • *Tell the picture story with your class.*

See Conversation Springboards on page 194.

_____   _____

_____

Partner Interview   Partner's Name _____

Practice these questions with your teacher. • _Then ask your partner._

1. What time do you get up in the morning?
2. What time do you eat breakfast?
3. What time do you eat lunch?
4. What time do you eat dinner?
5. How many hours is your English class?
6. How many hours do you sleep at night?

Group Survey

Ask everyone in your group these questions. • _Check YES or NO._ • _Count the answers._ • _Report your group's results to the class._ • _Write the class' results on the board._

Do you . . .	YES	NO
1. get up early in the morning?	_____	_____
2. get up before 7:00 a.m.?	_____	_____
3. go to bed late at night?	_____	_____
4. go to bed after midnight?	_____	_____
5. have an alarm clock?	_____	_____
6. come to class on time every day?	_____	_____
7. have lunch at noon?	_____	_____

EVERYDAY LIFE

A Mother's Day

A Worker's Day

1. do homework
2. do the laundry
3. feed the baby
4. get a paycheck
5. go shopping
6. go to school
7. go to work
8. make dinner
9. punch in
10. read to the children
11. sweep the floor
12. wash the dishes
13. work

_____
_____
_____
_____
_____

Class Discussion

Decide the correct time for each activity. • *Fill in the clocks.* • *Compare the everyday life of the mother and the worker.*

See Conversation Springboards on page 194.

Draw

Draw and write about your day.

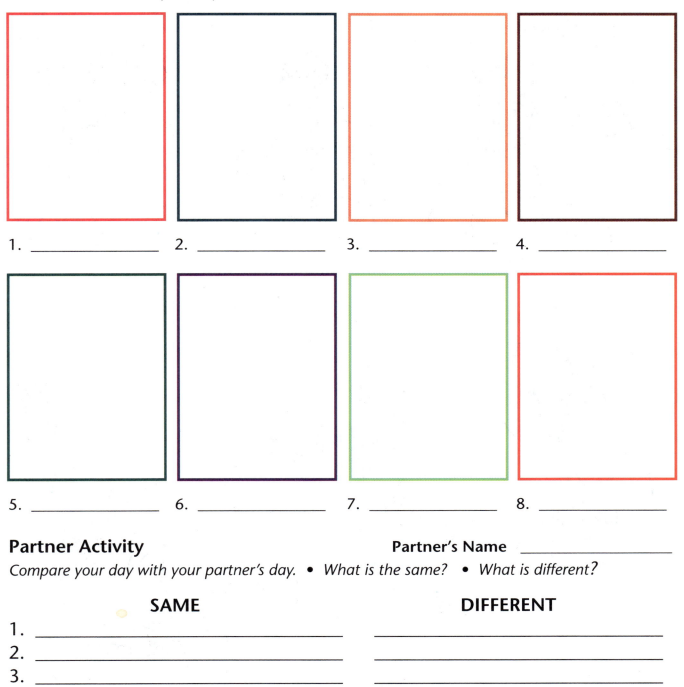

1. _____   2. _____   3. _____   4. _____

5. _____   6. _____   7. _____   8. _____

Partner Activity

Partner's Name _____

Compare your day with your partner's day. • *What is the same?* • *What is different?*

SAME	DIFFERENT
1. _____	_____
2. _____	_____
3. _____	_____

Find Someone Who

Review the vocabulary with your teacher. • *Fill in the name of someone who . . .*

1. _____ washes the dishes every evening.
2. _____ makes dinner at home.
3. _____ punches in at work.
4. _____ does the laundry.

21

MORNING ROUTINE

1. brush (his) teeth	5. get out of bed	9. say goodbye	_____
2. comb (his) hair	6. leave for work	10. shave	_____
3. drink coffee	7. make the bed	11. take a shower	_____
4. get dressed	8. read the newspaper	12. watch the news	_____

See Conversation Springboards on page 194.

What's the Story?

Work in groups of three. • Write a story about the man. • Everyone in the group should contribute three sentences. • Read your story to the class.

Group Game: *"What do you do in the morning?"*

Work in groups of five. • Pantomime a morning routine activity for your group. • No speaking! • Whoever guesses the activity takes the next turn.

REVIEW

Group Vocabulary Challenge

Work in groups of five. • *Make a list of all the vocabulary from your classroom.* • *Compare your list with another group.* • *Which group had the most new words?* • *Make a list of the new words on the board.* • *Copy the new words into your notebook.*

Class Activity

List ten questions about your day. • *Write them on the board.*

Partner Activity   Partner's Name _____

Ask your partner the questions from the Class Activity. • *Present your interview to the class.*

Partner Game: *"What do you do every day?"*   Partner's Name _____

Take turns. • *Pantomime what you do every day.* • *No speaking!* • *Let your partner guess.* • *List five of the activities.* • *Show your class what your partner does every day.*

THE CALENDAR

LEARNING STRATEGIES

➤ Make a calendar in English for this month. Write your activities on the calendar every day.

➤ In the Journal section of your notebook, write about the weather every day. For example, "Today the weather is . . ."

DAYS OF THE WEEK

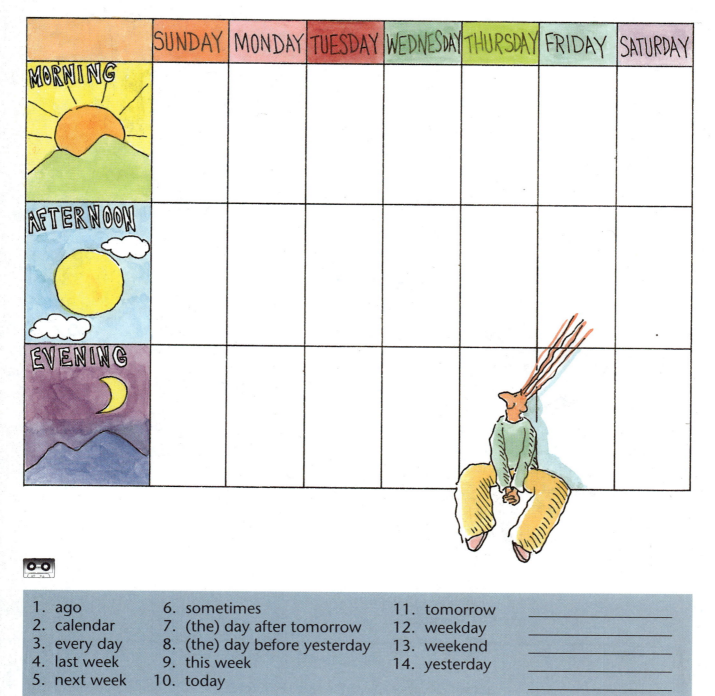

	SUNDAY	MONDAY	TUESDAY	WEDNESDAY	THURSDAY	FRIDAY	SATURDAY
MORNING							
AFTERNOON							
EVENING							

1. ago
2. calendar
3. every day
4. last week
5. next week
6. sometimes
7. (the) day after tomorrow
8. (the) day before yesterday
9. this week
10. today
11. tomorrow
12. weekday
13. weekend
14. yesterday

_____
_____
_____
_____
_____

Write

What are you doing every day this week? • *Fill in the calendar.* • *Explain it to your partner.*

26

See Conversation Springboards on pages 194 and 195.

Partner Interview

Practice these questions with your teacher. • *Then ask your partner.*

1. What is today?
2. What day is tomorrow?
3. What day was yesterday? What did you do yesterday?
4. What day was the day before yesterday?
5. What are you going to do next weekend?
6. What did you do last weekend?
7. Did you come to class last week?
8. Which is your favorite day? Why?
9. What are the days of the week?

Group Survey

Ask everyone in your group these questions. • *Check YES, NO, or SOMETIMES.* • *Count the answers.* • *Report your group's results to the class.* • *Write the class' results on the board.*

Do you . . .	YES	NO	SOMETIMES
1. sleep late on Sundays?	_____	_____	_____
2. shop on Saturday afternoons?	_____	_____	_____
3. study late in the evening?	_____	_____	_____
4. go to the movies on Friday evenings?	_____	_____	_____
5. work on the weekend?	_____	_____	_____

MONTHS AND DATES

JANUARY   FEBRUARY   MARCH   APRIL

MAY   JUNE   JULY   AUGUST

SEPTEMBER   OCTOBER   NOVEMBER   DECEMBER

1st (first)	12th (twelfth)	23rd (twenty-third)	century
2nd (second)	13th (thirteenth)	24th (twenty-fourth)	leap year
3rd (third)	14th (fourteenth)	25th (twenty-fifth)	year
4th (fourth)	15th (fifteenth)	26th (twenty-sixth)	_____
5th (fifth)	16th (sixteenth)	27th (twenty-seventh)	_____
6th (sixth)	17th (seventeenth)	28th (twenty-eighth)	
7th (seventh)	18th (eighteenth)	29th (twenty-ninth)	
8th (eighth)	19th (nineteenth)	30th (thirtieth)	
9th (ninth)	20th (twentieth)	31st (thirty-first)	
10th (tenth)	21st (twenty-first)		
11th (eleventh)	22nd (twenty-second)		

See Conversation Springboards on page 195.

Class Discussion

1. What's today's date?
2. What was last month?
3. What is next month?
4. What date does this course end?
5. What is the date of the next holiday?
6. When is the next leap year?
7. What century is this?

Group Activity

Work in groups of five or six. • *Decide on important dates.* • *Write them on your calendars.* • *Compare your dates with the rest of the class.*

Include:
1. your birthdays (or name days)
2. other important dates
3. important holidays in your countries

Class Game: *"What is your favorite month?"*

Think. • *Write.* • *Fold your paper.* • *Make a pile of papers.* • *Open one.* • *Read it to the class.* • *Guess who wrote it.*

BIRTHDAYS

1. balloon	8. gift	15. party _____
2. birthday cake	9. hide (র|이ᄃᆞ)	16. party hat _____
3. blow out the candles	10. horn	17. present _____
4. candle	11. knife	18. punch _____
5. celebrate	12. make a wish	19. spoon _____
6. cup	13. paper napkin	20. surprise _____
7. fork	14. paper plate	

What's the Story?

Work in groups of four. • *Write a story about the birthday party.* • *Everyone in the group should contribute at least one sentence.* • *Read your story to the class.*

1. What kind of celebration is this?
2. Whose birthday do you think it is?
3. How old is s/he?
4. What is on the table?
5. What do you think the presents are?

See Conversation Springboards on page 195.

Partner Interview

Practice these questions with your teacher. • *Then ask your partner.*

1. What do you like to give as a birthday gift to a friend? to a parent? to a co-worker? to a teacher? to a child?
2. When is your birthday? (or your name day?)
3. What kind of birthday cake is your favorite?
4. Describe how you like to celebrate your birthday (or your name day).

Write

Partner's Name _____

When is your partner's birthday? • *Write a message to your partner on the card.* • *Sign the birthday card.* • *Give it to your partner.* • *Read your message to your partner.*

Cross-Cultural Exchange

Do people celebrate birthdays or do they celebrate name days in your country? • *Tell the class how they celebrate.* • *How do you say "Happy Birthday" in your native language?* • *Teach it to the class.*

HOLIDAYS

Date: _____

Date: _____

Date: _____

Date: _____

1. band	6. fireworks	14. I love you!	22. Valentine's Day
2. champagne	7. flag	15. Independence Day	23. witch
3. chocolates	8. flowers	16. jack-o'-lantern	_____
4. costume	9. ghost	17. New Year's Eve	_____
5. decorations	10. Halloween	18. parade	_____
	11. Happy Halloween!	19. pumpkin	_____
	12. Happy New Year!	20. streamers	_____
	13. Happy Valentine's Day!	21. Trick or Treat!	_____

See Conversation Springboards on page 195.

Date: _____

Date: _____

1. apple pie
2. Christmas
3. Christmas lights
4. Merry Christmas!
5. Native Americans
6. Pilgrims
7. Santa Claus

8. settlers
9. Thanksgiving
10. tree
11. turkey
_____
_____
_____

Class Activity

Fill in the dates of this year's holidays with your class. • What is your favorite holiday? • Tell the class.

Conversation Squares

Work in groups of three. • First write your own answers. • Then ask your partners the questions. • Write their answers. • Compare your group's answers with other groups.

Favorite	You _____	Partner 1_____	Partner 2 _____
holiday	_____	_____	_____
holiday food	_____	_____	_____
holiday activity	_____	_____	_____

Cross-Cultural Exchange

How do you say "Merry Christmas" and "Happy New Year" in your native language? • Teach it to the class. • Make a list on the board. • Do you know a holiday song from your country? • Sing it for the class.

Speech

Tell the class about your favorite holiday. • Include the date, special activities, holiday food, and decorations.

See Conversation Springboards on page 195.

SEASONS

1. beach	8. farm stand	15. plow	22. summer
2. beach towel	9. garden	16. rake	23. tulip
3. bird	10. harvest	17. sled	24. volleyball
4. cider	11. ice	18. snow	25. water
5. cooler	12. ice skates	19. snowball	26. winter
6. egg	13. leaf	20. snowman	_____
7. fall (autumn)	14. nest	21. spring	_____

See Conversation Springboards on page 196.

Class Discussion

1. Where you live now, are the seasons the same as in the pictures?
2. What happens in each season?
3. What do you like to do in each season?
4. Which season is your favorite?
5. Are the seasons the same in your native city? What is different? What is the same?

What's the Story?

Work in groups of three. • Choose one season. • Write a story. • Everyone in the group should contribute at least two sentences. • Read your story to the class.

1. What are the people wearing?
2. What are they doing?
3. Do they like what they are doing?

Partner Game: *"What do you remember?"*   Partner's Name _____

Look at the picture with your partner. • Remember as much as you can. • Close your book. • Describe the picture with your partner. • List everything. • Compare your notes with another pair. • Add to your list.

WEATHER

1. bench	7. grass	13. nap	19. splash	25. umbrella
2. cactus	8. hail	14. picnic	20. storm	26. warm
3. clear	9. hailstorm	15. puddle	21. sun	27. wet
4. cloud	10. hill	16. rain	22. sunshine	28. wind
5. cowboy	11. horse	17. saddle	23. thunder	_____
6. dust storm	12. lightning	18. snowstorm	24. thunderstorm	_____

Class Discussion

What are the people in the pictures doing? • *What are they thinking?*

See Conversation Springboards on page 196.

Partner Interview

Practice these questions with your teacher. • *Then ask your partner.*

What do you like to do . . .

    1. on a rainy day?   3. on a cold day?

    2. on a sunny day?   4. on a snowy day?

Find Someone Who

Review the vocabulary with your teacher. • *Fill in the name of someone who . . .*

1. _____ never saw snow.
2. _____ was in a dust storm.
3. _____ was in a thunderstorm.
4. _____ likes rain.
5. _____ likes winter.
6. _____ likes to be outside in cold weather.
7. _____ likes to be outside in hot weather.
8. _____ was hit by hail.

37

WEATHER REPORT

1. cloudy	8. north	15. southeast	_____
2. cool	9. northeast	16. southwest	_____
3. dry	10. northwest	17. sunny	_____
4. east	11. rainy	18. temperature	_____
5. meteorologist	12. showers	19. weather map	_____
6. midwest	13. snowflakes	20. west	_____
7. mild	14. south	21. windy	_____

Group Activity

Work in groups of three. • Look at the weather map. • Report on the weather in the following areas. • Compare your answers with another group.

1. the Northeast
2. the Southeast
3. the Southwest
4. the Northwest
5. the Midwest

Community Activities

Bring in a weather report from either a native-language or an English newspaper. • Compare your report with others in the class.

Watch a weather report on TV. • Take notes:

1. What channel did you watch?
2. What time was the report on?
3. Who was the meteorologist?
4. What was the weather report for today?
5. Was it accurate?

See Conversation Springboards on page 196.

SEASONAL CLOTHING

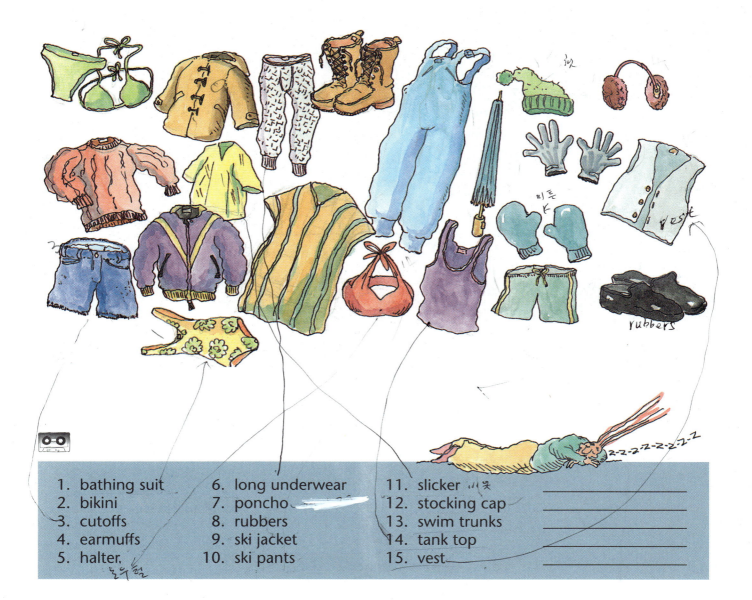

1. bathing suit
2. bikini
3. cutoffs
4. earmuffs
5. halter
6. long underwear
7. poncho
8. rubbers
9. ski jacket
10. ski pants
11. slicker
12. stocking cap
13. swim trunks
14. tank top
15. vest

Partner Interview

Partner's Name _____

Practice these questions with your teacher. • Then ask your partner.

1. What do you wear in cold weather?
2. What do you wear when it rains?
3. What do you wear in hot weather?
4. What do you wear when you go to the beach?
5. What do you wear when you go on a picnic?

Speech

Tell the class about the weather in your hometown. • Use these questions as a guide:

1. Are there seasons in your hometown? What are they? When are they?
2. What is the weather like in each season?
3. What do people wear in each season?

See Conversation Springboards on page 196.

39

REVIEW

Partner Interview

Practice these questions with your teacher. • *Then ask your partner.*

1. What is today's date?
2. What's the weather like today?
3. Is it hot? cold? warm? cool?
4. What season is it?
5. Do you like this weather?
6. What do you want to do today?

Write

Write in your journal.

Journal

_____
(1)

Today is a _____ day. It is
(2)

_____ during this season of _____.
(3)   (4)

I _____ the weather
(5)

today. It is a good day to _____.
(6)

Tell Your Partner

Read your journal entry to your partner. • *Listen to your partner's journal.*

40

NET. WT.
1.25 OZ.   CARVER ❀ FOTINOS

FOOD

LEARNING STRATEGIES

➤ Have lunch with one or more friends. Speak only English at lunch.

➤ Find food labels in English. Read the labels out loud. Ask your teacher about the pronunciation of new words.

FRUIT

1. apple
2. apricot
3. banana
4. blackberry
5. blueberry
6. box
7. bunch
8. buy
9. cantaloupe
10. cherry
11. coconut
12. grape
13. grapefruit
14. kiwi
15. lemon
16. lime
17. mango
18. orange
19. papaya
20. peach
21. pear
22. pineapple
23. pit
24. plum
25. pound
26. raspberry
27. seeds
28. skin
29. strawberry
30. watermelon

See Conversation Springboards on pages 196 and 197.

Partner Interview

Practice these questions with your teacher. • *Then ask your partner.*

1. What is your favorite kind of fruit?
2. What other fruit do you like?
3. What fruit grows in your country?
4. What fruit can you buy in your neighborhood?

Group Game: *"Preparing fruit salad"*

Work in groups of four. • *Prepare a fruit salad for the next class.*

To Get Ready:

What kind of fruit will each student bring?

_____   _____

_____   _____

Who will bring a bowl?   _____

Who will bring a knife?   _____

Who will bring a large spoon?   _____

Who will bring a fork?   _____

To Demonstrate:

• *Prepare your fruit salad.*

• *Compare the fruit salads.*

• *Vote on the best one.*

• *Enjoy the snack!*

43

VEGETABLES

1. artichoke	6. carrot	11. fresh	16. peas
2. bean	7. celery	12. head	17. pepper
3. beet	8. corn	13. lettuce	18. potato
4. broccoli	9. cucumber	14. mushroom	19. produce
5. cabbage	10. ear	15. onion	20. tomato

See Conversation Springboards on page 197.

Partner Interview

Practice these questions with your teacher. • *Then ask your partner.*

1. What is your favorite vegetable?
2. What vegetables don't you like?
3. What vegetables grow in your country?
4. Which vegetables do you usually use for salad?
5. What do fresh vegetables usually cost at your market?
6. Which vegetables do you buy by the bunch? by the head? by the ear? by the pound?

Group Decision

Work in groups of five or six. • *Decide which vegetables to use for a salad.* • *Decide how to prepare each vegetable.* • *Tell the class about your salad.*

VEGETABLE	YES/NO	COOKED	RAW	PEELED	SLICED	SHREDDED
	_____	_____	_____	_____	_____	_____
	_____	_____	_____	_____	_____	_____
	_____	_____	_____	_____	_____	_____
	_____	_____	_____	_____	_____	_____
	_____	_____	_____	_____	_____	_____
	_____	_____	_____	_____	_____	_____
	_____	_____	_____	_____	_____	_____
	_____	_____	_____	_____	_____	_____
other	_____	_____	_____	_____	_____	_____
TOTALS	_____	_____	_____	_____	_____	_____

45

MEAT, SEAFOOD, AND POULTRY

1. can
2. chicken
3. crab meat
4. fish
5. ground beef
6. ham
7. hot dogs
8. lamb chops
9. lamb roast
10. leg of lamb
11. liver
12. lobster
13. meatballs
14. octopus
15. package
16. pig's feet
17. pork chops
18. roast beef
19. sausages
20. shrimp
21. steak
22. stew beef
23. swordfish
24. tuna
25. tuna fish
_____
_____
_____

Partner Interview

Partner's Name _____

Practice these questions with your teacher. • *Then ask your partner.*

1. Do you eat meat? What is your favorite meat?
2. Do you eat poultry? What is your favorite?
3. Do you eat seafood? What is your favorite fish? What is your favorite shellfish?
4. Which meats, fish, and poultry are most common in your country?
5. Are there any meats, fish, or poultry that you never eat? Why?
6. Where do you buy meats? fish? poultry?
7. Is it a good idea to eat a lot of red meat? Why? Why not?

46   *See Conversation Springboards on page 197.*

1. bake
2. barbecue
3. boil
4. broil
5. casserole
6. fry
7. roast
8. seasoning
9. simmer
10. steam
11. stir fry

_____
_____
_____

Find Someone Who

How do you like your food prepared? • _Review the vocabulary with your teacher._ • _Fill in the name of someone who . . ._

1. _____ likes baked fish with salt and pepper.
2. _____ prepares barbecued spare ribs.
3. _____ doesn't eat fried food.
4. _____ knows how to prepare stir fry.
5. _____ likes meat simmered in sauce.
6. _____ likes casseroles.
7. _____ likes food with chili powder.
8. _____ broils steak with seasoning.

See Conversation Springboards on page 197.

DESSERTS

1. beverage	7. coffee	13. frozen yogurt	19. milkshake	25. tea
2. brownie	8. coffeecake	14. ice cream	20. pastry	_____
3. cake	9. cone	15. ice cream soda	21. pie	_____
4. candy	10. cookies	16. iced coffee	22. pie a la mode	_____
5. cappuccino	11. doughnut	17. iced tea	23. sherbet	_____
6. cheesecake	12. espresso	18. lemonade	24. sundae	_____

What's the Story?

Work in groups of five. • Choose one table. • Write a story about the people. • Everyone in the group should contribute at least two sentences. • Read your story to the class.

1. Who are the people?
2. Where are they?
3. What are they eating?

4. What are the children's favorite desserts?
5. What are the adults' favorite desserts?

See Conversation Springboards on page 197.

Group Discussion

Work in groups of five. • *Discuss these questions.* • *Report your answers to the class.*

1. What is your favorite dessert?
2. Do you buy it or prepare it?
3. How do you prepare it?
4. Is it fattening?
5. How often do you have your favorite dessert?

INTERNATIONAL DESSERT MENU

Group Role Play

Work in groups of five. • *First fill in this menu with the desserts your group likes.* • *Decide on prices.* • *Then write a role play ordering dessert and coffee (or tea) at a coffee shop.* • *Present your role play to the class.*

Cross-Cultural Exchange

Bring your favorite desserts or pastries to class. • *Take a break.* • *Have a dessert party.* • *Taste everyone's dessert!*

BREAKFAST

1. bacon	7. cream	13. home fries	19. oatmeal _____
2. bagel	8. cream cheese	14. jam	20. orange juice _____
3. butter	9. Danish	15. jelly	21. pancakes _____
4. cereal	10. French toast	16. margarine	22. sugar _____
5. cereal bowl	11. (fried) egg	17. milk	23. syrup _____
6. cocoa	12. grits	18. muffin	24. toast _____

Partner Interview

Partner's Name _____

Practice these questions with your teacher. • *Then ask your partner.*

1. What is a typical breakfast for you?
2. What time do you eat breakfast?
3. Do you eat breakfast with your family?
4. Do you eat breakfast at home?
5. In your opinion, what is a healthy breakfast?

50

See Conversation Springboards on page 198.

Cross-Cultural Exchange

What do people usually eat for breakfast in your country? • *Tell the class.* • *Add new vocabulary to the list.*

Conversation Squares

Work in groups of three. • *First write your own answers.* • *Then ask your partners the questions.* • *Write their answers.* • *Compare your group's answers with other groups.*

Breakfast	You _____	Partner 1_____	Partner 2 _____
today	_____	_____	_____
yesterday	_____	_____	_____
tomorrow	_____	_____	_____

Group Survey

Ask everyone in your group these questions. • *Check ALWAYS, SOMETIMES, or NEVER.* • *Count the answers.* • *Report your group's results to the class.* • *Write the class' results on the board.*

How often do you . . .	ALWAYS	SOMETIMES	NEVER
1. skip breakfast?	_____	_____	_____
2. drink coffee for breakfast?	_____	_____	_____
3. have cold cereal for breakfast?	_____	_____	_____
4. have hot cereal for breakfast?	_____	_____	_____
5. have fruit or juice for breakfast?	_____	_____	_____
6. have something sweet for breakfast?	_____	_____	_____
7. eat out for breakfast?	_____	_____	_____
8. eat a nutritious breakfast?	_____	_____	_____

LUNCH

1. boiled ham	12. ketchup	23. roll	27. slice of bread
2. bologna	13. leftovers	24. salad	28. soup
3. bread	14. lunch box	25. salami	29. spaghetti
4. brown paper bag/sack	15. lunchroom	26. sandwich	30. spaghetti sauce
5. cafeteria	16. mayonnaise		31. thermos
6. cheese	17. microwave oven		32. yogurt
7. coffee mug	18. mustard		
8. cold cuts	19. peanut butter		
9. frozen entree	20. plastic baggie		
10. ham sandwich	21. potato chips		
11. hero (submarine/grinder)	22. roast beef sandwich		

What's the Story?

Work in groups of five. • *Choose one scene and write a story.* • *Everyone in the group should contribute at least two sentences.* • *Read your story to the class.*

1. Where are the people?
2. What are their names?
3. What are they eating and drinking?
4. What are they saying?

See Conversation Springboards on page 198.

Partner Interview

Practice these questions with your teacher. • *Then ask your partner.*

1. What time do you usually eat lunch?
2. Where do you eat lunch?
3. What do you usually eat for lunch?
4. What do you usually drink for lunch?
5. Do you usually eat a nutritious lunch?
6. Do you ever skip lunch? Why?
7. Do you bring your lunch to work? to school? What do you bring?
8. Do you make your own lunch? If not, who makes it for you?
9. If you buy your lunch, where do you buy it? How much does it cost?
10. Who do you usually eat lunch with? What do you talk about?

Write

What is your favorite sandwich? • *How do you prepare it?* • *Write the recipe.* • *Tell the class how to make your favorite sandwich.*

Recipe

_____
(1)

Spread _____ on
(2)

_____.
(3)

Put _____ on the bread
(4)
and close the sandwich.

Cut in half.
Enjoy the sandwich!

Choose one:

(1) roast beef sandwich
 peanut butter & jelly
 tuna fish sandwich
 ham & cheese sandwich
 other:_____

(2) mayonnaise
 butter
 margarine
 mustard
 ketchup
 peanut butter
 other:_____

(3) rye bread
 white bread
 wheat bread
 a roll
 other:_____

(4) roast beef
 tuna fish
 ham and cheese
 jelly
 other:_____

FAST FOOD

1. bun	7. customer	13. pay	19. straw
2. cashier	8. drive-in/drive-thru window	14. pickle	_____
3. cash register	9. hamburger	15. salad bar	_____
4. change	10. hot sauce (salsa)	16. salad dressing	_____
5. chicken nuggets	11. line	17. shake	_____
6. counter	12. order	18. soft drink	_____

54

See Conversation Springboards on page 198.

Group Survey

Ask everyone in your group these questions. • *Check YES or NO.* • *Count the answers.* • *Report your group's results to the class.* • *Write the class' results on the board.*

Do you . . .	YES	NO
1. ever eat fast foods?	_____	_____
2. like hamburgers with "everything"?	_____	_____
3. like French fries?	_____	_____
4. like ketchup on your fries?	_____	_____
5. like chicken nuggets?	_____	_____
6. like hot dogs?	_____	_____
7. like mustard on your hot dogs?	_____	_____
8. like soft drinks?	_____	_____
9. like salsa?	_____	_____
10. think fast food is bad for you?	_____	_____

Partner Role Play

With your partner, complete this role play. • *Present your role play to the class.*

Cashier: May I help you?
Customer: _____

Cashier: Anything to drink?
Customer: _____

Cashier: Anything else?
Customer: _____

Cashier: That'll be $ _____.__, please.

Customer: Here's _____

     [Customer gives cashier $20.00.]

Cashier: That's $_____ change. Have a nice day.

     [Cashier takes out change from the cash register, and gives change to customer.]

55

JUNK FOOD

1. bubble gum	6. crackers	11. pretzels	_____
2. candy bar	7. gum	12. snack machine	_____
3. cheese snack	8. juice drink	13. soda	_____
4. chocolate bar	9. peanuts	14. tortilla chips	_____
5. corn chips	10. popcorn	15. vending machine	_____

Class Discussion

1. Which junk foods do you like? Which don't you like?
2. Do you ever eat junk food? When?
3. Where do you buy junk food?

Class Game: *"What is your favorite junk food?"*

Write the name of your favorite junk food. • Fold your paper. • Make a pile. • Open one. • Guess who wrote it. • Who likes the same junk food?

Group Decision

Work in groups of five or six. • Your group has $5.00 to spend on snacks. • Look at the picture. • What will you buy from the snack machines? • Tell the class.

See Conversation Springboards on page 198.

DINNER

1. ash tray
2. beer
3. busboy
4. check
5. glass of water
6. hostess
7. maitre d'
8. nonsmoking section
9. restaurant
10. restroom
11. smoking section _____
12. tip _____
13. waiter _____
14. waitress _____
15. wine _____

What's the Story?

Work in groups of five. • *Write a story about one of the tables in the picture.* • *Everyone in the group should contribute at least one sentence.* • *Read your story to the class.*

1. Who are the people? What are their names?
2. Why are they going out to eat tonight?
3. What are they having for dinner?
4. How are they feeling tonight?
5. What are they saying?
6. Who will pay the check?
7. What will they do after they leave the restaurant?

See Conversation Springboards on pages 198 and 199.

THE SUPERMARKET

1. aisle	6. checkout counter	11. loaf	16. tomato paste
2. bottle	7. courtesy desk	12. rice	17. whipped cream
3. bottle return	8. dozen	13. section	_____
4. can return	9. grated cheese	14. shelf	_____
5. carton	10. jar	15. shopping cart	_____

Group Vocabulary Challenge

Work in groups of four. • List as many supermarket items as you can. • Compare your list with another group.

Group Decision

Work in groups of three or four. • Compare these jars of tomato sauce. • Tell the class about your findings.

32 oz. $2.19

24 oz. $1.49

8 oz. $ .59

largest	_____	_____	_____
smallest	_____	_____	_____
most expensive	_____	_____	_____
cheapest	_____	_____	_____
best buy	_____	_____	_____

See Conversation Springboards on page 199.

Community Activity

Review this list with your teacher. • *Add two items.* • *Go to your supermarket.* • *Fill out the chart.* • *In the next class, compare your charts.*

Supermarket Name: _____

ITEM	SIZE	BRAND NAME	PRICE
1. bread	_____	_____	_____
2. coffee	_____	_____	_____
3. rice	_____	_____	_____
4. _____	_____	_____	_____
5. _____	_____	_____	_____

REVIEW

Group Decision

Work in groups of five or six. • Choose one of the family pictures. • Plan menus for one day (breakfast, lunch, dinner, and snacks) for the family. • Figure the cost.

Breakfast

_____
_____
_____   } $_____
_____

Lunch

_____
_____
_____   } $_____
_____

Dinner

_____
_____
_____   } $_____
_____

Snacks

_____
_____
_____   } $_____
_____

Class Game: *"What is it?"*

Choose a leader.

> **Leader:** *Think of a food you like. Don't say it!*
> **Class:** *Ask the leader YES/NO questions.*
> **Leader:** *Answer "Yes" or "No."*
> **Class:** *Try to guess the food. Whoever guesses is the new leader.*

Cross-Cultural Exchange

Bring special foods from your country to class. • Have an international party. • Bring music from your country to play at the party. • Enjoy!

HOMES

LEARNING STRATEGIES

➤ Make labels in English for everything in your home. Repeat the new vocabulary every time you look at a label.

➤ With a classmate, describe each room in your home. Then compare your homes.

CITY OR COUNTRY

1. beautiful	6. desert	11. live	16. rural
2. busy	7. exciting	12. mountain	17. suburban
3. calm	8. farm	13. noisy	_____
4. coast	9. grow up	14. peaceful	_____
5. crowded	10. jungle	15. ranch	_____

Partner Interview

Partner's Name _____

Practice these questions with your teacher. • *Then ask your partner.*

1. Where do you live now?
2. How long have you lived there?
3. Where were you born?
4. Where did you grow up?
5. Where do you want to live?

See Conversation Springboards on page 199.

Group Discussion

Work in groups of three. • Discuss these questions. • Report your answers to the class.
1. Do you like where you live now?
2. In your opinion, where is the best place in the world to live?
3. Decide as a group which place you like best. Tell your class why. If you can't agree on a place, tell your class why you can't agree.

Speech

Bring in a picture or a photo of a beautiful place to live. • Tell the class about the picture. • Use these questions as a guide.
1. Where is the place?
2. Why do you think it is beautiful?
3. Why do you want to live there?

Group Game: *"Gossip!"*

Work in groups of eight. • Choose a leader. • Close your books. • Look at the cover. • What are the people saying?

Leader: [*To the first student*] Read the secret on page 247. Close your book. Whisper the secret to the student sitting next to you.

That Student: [*Whisper the secret to the student sitting next to you, etc.*]

Last Student: [*Write the secret on the board or tell the class.*]

Class: [*Check the secret on page 247. Which group had the most accurate secret?*]

HOMES

1. apartment (flat)	9. chimney	17. prison (prizn) _____
2. attic	10. condominium	18. private home _____
3. awning	11. dormitory	19. roof _____
4. balcony	12. fence	20. steps _____
5. basement	13. garage	21. stucco _____
6. brick	14. house	22. terrace _____
7. cactus garden	15. mobile home	23. wood _____
8. cement	16. porch	24. yard _____

What's the Story?

Work in groups of three. • Decide which home to describe. • Write a story about the home and the people. • Everyone in the group should contribute at least two sentences. • Read your story to the class.

See Conversation Springboards on pages 199 and 200.

Conversation Squares

Work in groups of four. • *First write your own answers.* • *Then ask your partners the questions.* • *Write their answers.* • *Compare your group's answers with other groups.* • *Make a class directory.*

1. What's your name? First/Middle/Last: _____ **What's your address?** Number/Street _____ Apartment number _____ City or Town _____ State _____ ZIP Code _____ **What's your phone number?** Area Code: (_____) Number: _____	**3. What's your name?** First/Middle/Last: _____ **What's your address?** Number/Street _____ Apartment number _____ City or Town _____ State _____ ZIP Code _____ **What's your phone number?** Area Code: (_____) Number: _____
2. What's your name? First/Middle/Last: _____ **What's your address?** Number/Street _____ Apartment number _____ City or Town _____ State _____ ZIP Code _____ **What's your phone number?** Area Code: (_____) Number: _____	**4. What's your name?** First/Middle/Last: _____ **What's your address?** Number/Street _____ Apartment number _____ City or Town _____ State _____ ZIP Code _____ **What's your phone number?** Area Code: (_____) Number: _____

THE KITCHEN

1. burner
2. cabinet
3. can opener
4. coffee maker
5. creamer
6. cupboard
7. dishpan
8. dishwasher
9. dryer
10. electric mixer
11. faucet
12. freezer
13. frying pan
14. linoleum
15. oven
16. pot
17. refrigerator
18. sink
19. small appliance
20. stove
21. sugar bowl
22. tea kettle
23. toaster
24. washing machine
25. wok
_____
_____
_____
_____
_____
_____
_____

See Conversation Springboards on page 200.

What's the Story?

Work in groups of five. • Write a story about the kitchen. • Everyone in the group should contribute at least two sentences. • Read your story to the class.

1. Where is the family?
2. What are their names?
3. What time is it?
4. What is the family doing?

Partner Game: *"Same or Different?"*

Partner's Name _____

One partner looks at the picture on this page. • The other partner looks at the picture on page 66. • Compare kitchens. • List everything in both kitchens. • What is the same? • What is different?

SAME   **DIFFERENT**

1: _____   _____
2. _____   _____
3. _____   _____

THE DINING ROOM

1. candlestick
2. glass
3. napkin
4. pepper shaker
5. pie server
6. pitcher
7. plate
8. salad bowl
9. salt shaker
10. saucer
11. serving spoon
12. set the table
13. silverware
14. soup bowl
15. tablecloth
16. tablespoon
17. teaspoon
18. vase

_____
_____
_____
_____
_____
_____

See Conversation Springboards on page 200.

Partner Interview

Practice these questions with your teacher. • *Then ask your partner.*

1. What room do you eat in at home?
2. How do you set the table at home? for breakfast? lunch? dinner?
3. Does your family always eat together?

Group Activity

Work in groups of four or five. • *With your group, list five things people say at the dinner table.* • *Read your list to the class.* • *Make a list on the board.*

Group Role Play

Work in groups of five. • *Choose one scene.* • *Write a role play with your group.* • *Include roles for everyone.* • *Present your role play to the class.*

1. a family eating together
2. a family setting the table for dinner with guests
3. a teenager eating with his or her friends in the kitchen

Include in your role play:

1. the people (Give them names!)
2. how they feel
3. what they are saying
4. what is on the table
5. the food

Cross-Cultural Exchange

What are some traditional eating customs in your country? • *Tell the class.* • *How are the customs the same in different countries?* • *Which countries are the most similar?*

69

THE LIVING ROOM

1. armchair	8. lamp	15. radio	22. television (TV)
2. bookcase	9. lampshade	16. read a book	23. throw pillow
3. CD player	10. laser disc player	17. relax	24. VCR
4. coffee table	11. listen to music	18. rug	25. watch TV
5. drapes	12. magazine	19. sofa (couch)	_____
6. fireplace	13. photograph	20. speakers	_____
7. furniture	14. plant	21. stereo	_____

Group Vocabulary Challenge

Work in groups of four. • *Make a list of everything you do in your living rooms.* • *Read your list to the class.* • *Which group had the most new words?* • *Make a list on the board.* • *Copy the new words into your notebook.*

See Conversation Springboards on pages 200 and 201.

Class Game: *"What do you do in the living room?"*

Think. • Write an activity. • Fold your paper. • Make a pile of papers. • Open one. • Follow the instruction. • Ask "What am I doing?" • Have the class guess the activity.

Group Game: *"Gossip!"*

Work in groups of eight. • Choose a leader. • Close your books. • Look at the cover. • What are the people saying?

Leader:	[*To the first student*] Read the secret on page 247. Close your book. Whisper the secret to the student sitting next to you.
That Student:	[*Whisper the secret to the student sitting next to you, etc.*]
Last Student:	[*Write the secret on the board or tell the class.*]
Class:	[*Check the secret on page 247. Which group had the most accurate secret?*]

Community Activity

Bring in ads from stores that sell furniture. • Decide as a class how to furnish a living room. • What will you buy? • How much will each item cost? • What will the total bill be?

bill

THE BEDROOM

1. bedspread	8. comb	15. pillow
2. blanket	9. curtains	16. pillowcase
3. box spring	10. drawer	17. shade
4. brush	11. dresser	18. sheets
5. carpet	12. mattress	19. telephone
6. chest of drawers	13. mirror	20. vanity
7. closet	14. night stand	

See Conversation Springboards on page 201.

Class Game: *"What do you remember?"*

Look at the picture. • *Remember as much as you can.* • *Close your book.* • *List everything.* •
Compare your answers with the class. • *Who had the longest list?* • *Open your book and check
your answers.*

Partner Interview

Partner's Name _____

Practice these questions with your teacher. • *Then ask your partner.*

Do you remember your childhood bedroom?

1. How many windows did it have?
2. How many doors did it have?
3. What furniture was in the room?
4. Where did you keep your clothes?
5. What toys did you have in your bedroom?
6. What was on the walls?
7. What was on the floor?
8. What did you see from the window?
9. Did you like your bedroom? Why or why not?

Draw

Draw a picture of your childhood bedroom. • *Explain your picture to your partner.*

THE BATHROOM

	8. deodorant	17. shower	26. toothpaste
	9. drain	18. shower curtain	27. towel
1. aspirin	10. electric razor	19. soap	_____
2. bandaid	11. hand towel	20. soap dish	_____
3. bath towel	12. mat	21. tiles	_____
4. bath toy	13. medicine cabinet	22. toilet	_____
5. bathtub	14. razor	23. toilet paper	_____
6. bubble bath	15. shampoo	24. toilet seat	_____
7. conditioner	16. shaving cream	25. toothbrush	_____

What's the Story?

Work in groups of three. • Write a story about the bathroom. • Everyone in the group should contribute at least three sentences. • Read your story to the class.

1. What time of day is it?
2. Who are the people?
3. What are their names?
4. What are they doing?
5. What are they going to do?
6. What are they thinking?

Cross-Cultural Exchange

Are baths or showers more popular in your country? • Is the toilet in the same room as the bath? • Do children use training toilets? • Do people sing in the shower? the bath?

See Conversation Springboards on page 201.

AT HOME

Class Vocabulary Challenge

Look at the picture. • What do you see in this home? • Make a list of the vocabulary words you can remember. • Read your list to the class. • Who has the most new words? • Make a list on the board. • Copy the new words into your notebook.

Group Survey 🔲

Ask everyone in your group these questions. • Check EVERY DAY, SOMETIMES, or NEVER. • Count the answers. • Report your group's results to the class. • Write the class' results on the board.

How often do you . . .	EVERY DAY	SOMETIMES	NEVER
1. eat lunch at home?	_____	_____	_____
2. watch TV in the evening?	_____	_____	_____
3. read magazines in the bathtub?	_____	_____	_____
4. write letters in the kitchen?	_____	_____	_____
5. talk on the telephone?	_____	_____	_____
6. take care of children?	_____	_____	_____
7. sing in the shower?	_____	_____	_____
8. cook your own meals?	_____	_____	_____
9. sleep well at night?	_____	_____	_____

🔲 *See Conversation Springboards on page 201.*

NEIGHBORS

1. baby-sit	6. friendly	11. next door
2. borrow	7. gossip	12. problem
3. bother	8. have a party	13. secret
4. chat	9. help	14. unfriendly
5. fight	10. lend	15. whisper

See Conversation Springboards on page 201.

Partner Interview

Partner's Name _____

Practice these questions with your teacher. • *Then ask your partner.*

1. How many neighbors do you know?
2. Are your neighbors friendly?
3. What languages do your neighbors speak?
4. Do you visit your neighbors?
5. Do the children in your neighborhood play together? What games do they play?
6. Do the children ever fight?
7. Do you have any problems with your neighbors? What kind of problems?

Group Role Play

Work in groups of four or five. • *Choose one scene.* • *Write a role play with your group.* • *Include roles for everyone.* • *Present your role play to the class.*

PROBLEMS AT HOME

1. cockroach
2. drip
3. exterminator
4. flooded
5. freezing
6. leak
7. leaking roof

8. mouse
9. (no) heat
10. off
11. on
12. overflow
13. pest
14. pesticide

15. plugged up/
    stopped up
16. plunger
17. radiator
18. shiver

_____
_____
_____
_____
_____
_____
_____

See Conversation Springboards on page 202.

Group Problem Posing/Problem Solving

Work in groups of five. • State the problems. • Give advice to the people. • Suggest solutions. • Read your problems and solutions to the class.

Group Role Play

Work in groups of five. • Choose one scene. • Write a role play with your group. • Include roles for everyone. • Present your role play to the class.

Strip Stories

Discuss these stories with your class. • State the problems. • What mistakes are they making? • Write captions.

Group Activity

Work in groups of five. • Make a list of problems you have at home. • Read your list to the class. • Compare lists. • What is the biggest problem? • Make a list on the board. • Copy the new words into your notebook. • Discuss solutions for all the problems.

REVIEW

Partner Interview

Partner's Name _____

Practice these questions with your teacher. • *Then ask your partner.*

1. What is today's date?
2. What is your name?
3. Where do you live?
4. How many rooms are in your home?
5. Where do you study?

6. Where do you watch TV?
7. Where do you eat breakfast?
8. Do you know your neighbors?
9. Do you like your neighbors?
10. Why?

Write

Write about your partner.

Journal

_____
(1)

My partner's name is _____. My
(2)

partner lives in _____. S/he
(3)

has _____ rooms in his/her home. S/he
(4)

studies in the _____.
(5)

S/he watches TV in the _____.
(6)

S/he eats breakfast in the _____.
(7)

S/he _____ his/her neighbors.
(8)

S/he _____ the neighbors because
(9)

_____.
(10)

Tell the Class

Read your journal to the class. • *Tell the class about your partner.*

80

UNIT 6

SHOPPING

LEARNING STRATEGIES

➤ Write all your shopping lists in English. Go shopping with a friend from class. Shop in English.

➤ Show your purchases to classmates. Describe your purchases in English. Ask questions about what your classmates bought.

GOING SHOPPING!

1. coffee shop (cafe)
2. department store
3. electronics store
4. flower stand
5. hardware store
6. jewelry store
7. mall
8. men's clothing store
9. music store
10. pharmacy
11. shoe store
12. shopping center
13. sporting goods store
14. stationery store
15. toy store
16. women's clothing store

_____
_____
_____
_____
_____
_____

See Conversation Springboards on page 202.

Class Activity

Are these stores in your neighborhood? • Write the names of your neighborhood stores on the signs. • What do you buy in each of the stores? • Make a list on the board of three items for each store.

Group Discussion

Work in groups of five. • Discuss these questions. • Report your answers to the class.

1. Where do you shop?
2. When do you go shopping?
3. What stores do you go to?
4. Which stores in your neighborhood do you like best? Why?
5. Which store do you recommend to the class?

SPORTING GOODS STORE

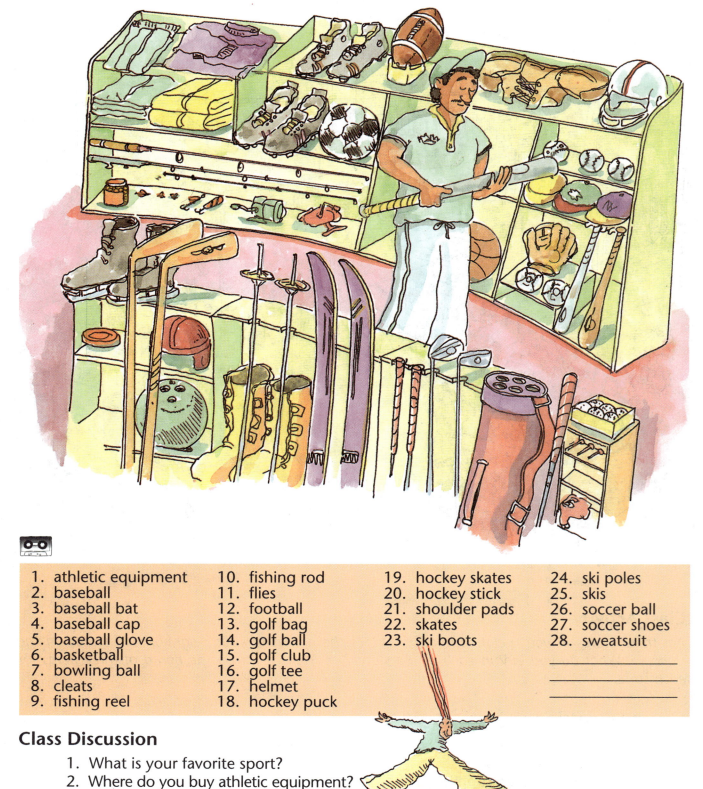

1. athletic equipment
2. baseball
3. baseball bat
4. baseball cap
5. baseball glove
6. basketball
7. bowling ball
8. cleats
9. fishing reel

10. fishing rod
11. flies
12. football
13. golf bag
14. golf ball
15. golf club
16. golf tee
17. helmet
18. hockey puck

19. hockey skates
20. hockey stick
21. shoulder pads
22. skates
23. ski boots

24. ski poles
25. skis
26. soccer ball
27. soccer shoes
28. sweatsuit

_____
_____
_____

Class Discussion

1. What is your favorite sport?
2. Where do you buy athletic equipment?
3. What do you buy?
4. Is it expensive? How much does it cost?
5. What kind of clothing do you buy in a sporting goods store?

See Conversation Springboards on page 202.

Group Decision

Work in groups of four. • Decide what to buy for one of the following situations. • Report your decisions to the class.

1. Your ten-year-old nephew is having a birthday. He is on a baseball team for the first time.
2. Your sister and brother-in-law are having an anniversary. Your sister likes to play golf. Your brother-in-law likes to bowl.
3. You live in a warm climate. You want to take up a new sport.

Group Vocabulary Challenge

Work in groups of four. • Make a list of special equipment you need for these sports. • Read your list to the class. • Which group had the most new words? • Make a list on the board. • Copy the list into your notebook.

skiing   baseball

golf   hockey

ice skating   basketball

bowling   other: _____

Find Someone Who

Review the vocabulary with your teacher. • Fill in the name of someone who . . .

1. _____ has a sweatsuit.
2. _____ is wearing sneakers.
3. _____ bought a new soccer ball.
4. _____ works at a sporting goods store.
5. _____ likes to wear a baseball cap.
6. _____ would like to buy golf clubs.

TOY STORE

1. bicycle	7. doll	13. paint set	19. toy kitchen
2. board game	8. duck	14. penguin	20. tricycle
3. car	9. electric train	15. rubber ball	21. truck
4. chess set	10. fire engine	16. snake	
5. computer game	11. mobile	17. stuffed animal	
6. darts	12. model airplane	18. teddy bear	

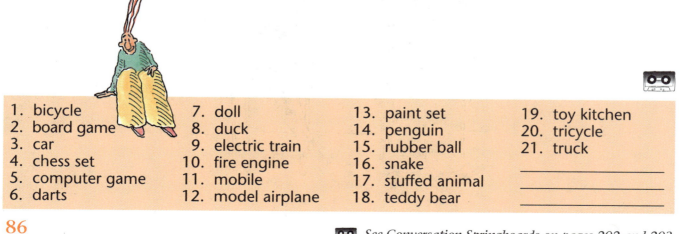

See Conversation Springboards on pages 202 and 203.

Partner Interview

Practice these questions with your teacher. • *Then ask your partner.*

1. When you were a child, did you have a favorite toy? What was it?
2. What children's toys were popular in your country when you were a child? What is popular now?
3. What do children like to play with where you live now?
4. Do you buy toys? Where do you buy them?

Group Decision

Work in groups of four. • *Decide what toy to buy for each of these children.* • *Report your decisions to the class.*

1. a baby girl
2. a two-year-old boy
3. an eight-year-old boy
4. a five-year-old girl
5. a ten-year-old girl

Group Survey

Ask everyone in your group these questions. • *Check YES or NO.* • *Count the answers.* • *Report your group's results to the class.* • *Write the class' results on the board.*

When you were a child . . .	YES	NO
1. did you ever play with dolls?	_____	_____
2. did you ever ride a tricycle?	_____	_____
3. did you like to color?	_____	_____
4. did you like to play ball?	_____	_____
5. did you like to read?	_____	_____

SHOE STORE

1. baby shoes
2. canvas
3. cheap
4. expensive
5. fit
6. flats
7. heel
8. high heels
9. leather
10. length
11. loafers
12. man-made materials
13. moccasins
14. narrow (N)
15. plastic
16. rubber boots
17. shoe box
18. shoe horn
19. shoe polish
20. shoe size
21. shoe tree
22. sole
23. suede
24. walking shoes
25. Western boots
26. wide (W)
27. width
28. winter boots
29. work boots
_____
_____
_____

Group Role Play

Work in groups of five. • *Write a role play for the scene.* • *Include roles for everyone.* • *Present your role play to the class.*

See Conversation Springboards on page 203.

Find Someone Who

Review the vocabulary with your teacher. • *Fill in the name of someone who . . .*

1. _____ has more than ten pairs of shoes.
2. _____ wants Western boots.
3. _____ buys expensive shoes.
4. _____ wears the same size shoes as you do.
5. _____ has more than one pair of work shoes.

Group Discussion

Work in groups of five. • *Discuss these questions.* • *Report your answers to the class.*

1. How many pairs of shoes do you have?
2. Where do you buy your shoes?
3. What shoes do you wear to work?
4. What shoes do you wear to school?
5. What shoes do you wear to go dancing?
6. What kind of shoes do you wear in cold weather?
7. Which shoes are your favorite shoes?
8. What is your shoe size?

Cross-Cultural Exchange

What kinds of shoes are popular in your country? • *Are shoe sizes in your country different from shoe sizes in the United States?* • *Are shoes made in your country?* • *What kinds?*

MEN'S CLOTHING STORE

1. bathrobe	5. extra large (XL)	9. short sleeves	13. undershirt
2. cap	6. large (L)	10. small (S)	14. wallet
3. casual wear	7. long sleeves	11. sweat pants	_____
4. dress shirt	8. medium (M)	12. turtleneck	_____

Partner Interview

Partner's Name _____

Practice these questions with your teacher. • *Then ask your partner.*

1. Where is the men's store in your neighborhood?
2. What can you buy in the store?
3. When do you shop for men's clothes?
4. Who do you buy men's clothing for?

Group Decision

Work in groups of five or six. • *Decide what clothing the men in the picture will buy for the following activities.* • *Report your decisions to the class.*

1. jogging
2. a job interview
3. a wedding
4. fixing a car
5. going to a movie
6. going to class

See Conversation Springboards on page 203.

WOMEN'S CLOTHING STORE

1. bra/brassiere
2. clothing rack
3. hat rack
4. headband
5. hosiery
6. nightgown
7. price tag
8. robe
9. shopping bag
10. slacks (pants)
11. slip
12. tights
13. try on
_____
_____
_____

Partner Vocabulary Challenge
Partner's Name _____

Make a list of the other vocabulary words in this picture. • *How many words do you remember?*
• *Compare your list with another pair of students.* • *Add to your list.*

Group Decision

Work in groups of five or six. • *With your group, decide what one of these women will buy today.* •
Report your decisions to the class.

1. What is her name?
2. Why is she shopping today?
3. What will she try on?
4. What new clothes will she buy?
5. How much money will she spend?
6. How will she pay for the clothes?

Community Activity

Bring in newspaper ads for women's clothing. • *Choose one item to buy.* • *How much does it
cost?* • *Make a list on the board of the items everyone in the class wants to buy.* • *List the
prices.* • *Who wanted the most expensive item? the least expensive?* • *What was the most
popular item?*

See Conversation Springboards on page 203.

DEPARTMENT STORE

1. appliances	7. gift wrap	13. men's room
2. cosmetics	8. home entertainment	14. store directory
3. domestics	9. home furnishings	15. toy department
4. electronics	10. jewelry counter	16. women's department
5. elevator	11. ladies' room	
6. escalator	12. men's department	

Class Discussion

1. Is there a department store in your neighborhood? Where?
2. Do you shop there? What do you buy?
3. Which is your favorite department store? Why do you like it?
4. Are department stores the same or different in your country? Tell the class.

92

See Conversation Springboards on pages 203 and 204.

Partner Game: *"What do you remember?"*   Partner's Name _____

*Look at the picture with your partner. • Remember as much as you can. • Close your book. •
Describe the picture. • List everything. • Compare your list with another pair. • Add to your list.*

Partner Role Play   Partner's Name _____

*With your partner, write role plays for three of these situations. • Present your role plays to
the class.*

You are at the escalator and want to get to . . .

  1. the gift wrap counter.
  2. the toy department.
  3. the jewelry department.
  4. the returns counter.
  5. the men's department.

FLOWER SHOP

1. bouquet	7. daffodil	13. gardenia	18. lily	24. stem
2. bud	8. daisy	14. geranium	19. orchid	25. thorn
3. carnation	9. fern	15. gladiola	20. petal	26. wreath
4. corsage	10. floral arrangement	16. hanging	21. philodendron	_____
5. crocus	11. florist	plant	22. pot	_____
6. cut flowers	12. flower pot	17. iris	23. rose	_____

See Conversation Springboards on page 204.

What's the Story?

Work in groups of three or four. • *Tell the story of each person in the flower shop.* • *Everyone in the group should contribute at least two sentences.* • *Read your story to the class.*

1. Who are the people? What are their names?
2. What occasions are they buying flowers for?
3. What are they going to do when they leave the shop?

Partner Role Play   Partner's Name _____

With your partner, choose one situation. • *Write a role play.* • *Present your conversation to the class.*

1. You are buying flowers for your 85-year-old grandmother's birthday. What do you buy? How much do you want to spend? What will you write on the card?
2. Your friend is in the hospital. You want to buy some flowers or a plant to take when you visit. How much do you want to spend? What do you want to buy? What will you write on the card?
3. It's the last day of class. You are buying a plant for your teacher. How much money did you collect? What will you buy? Will you have the florist put a ribbon around the plant? What color? What will you write on the card?

Class Discussion

1. What is your favorite flower? Why do you like it?
2. Is there a flower shop in your neighborhood? Where? What can you buy?
3. When do you buy flowers?
4. How can you send flowers?
5. When do people give flowers and plants in your country?

PHARMACY

1. antacid	6. hair spray	11. mouthwash	16. tissues
2. cold medicine	7. lip gloss	12. nail polish	17. vitamins
3. cough syrup	8. lipstick	13. pharmacist	_____
4. diapers	9. makeup	14. skin lotion	_____
5. film	10. medicine	15. sunscreen	_____

Group Vocabulary Challenge

Work in groups of four or five. • Make a list of everything you buy at the pharmacy. • Compare your list with another group. • Which group had the most new words? • List the new words on the board. • Copy the new words into your notebook.

See Conversation Springboards on page 204.

Class Survey

Take a survey. • Use the list on the board. • How many students buy the items at the pharmacy? • Write the total next to each item. • What do most students buy?

Conversation Squares

Work in groups of three. • First write your own answers. • Then ask your partners the questions. • Write their answers. • Compare your group's answers with other groups.

Brand	You _____	Partner 1_____	Partner 2_____
	_____	_____	_____
	_____	_____	_____
	_____	_____	_____
	_____	_____	_____
	_____	_____	_____

Community Activity

Compare the prices for the following items in two different stores. • Report the results to the class.

ITEM	STORE:_____	STORE:_____
soap: brand _____		
size: _____	Price $_____	Price $_____
shampoo: brand _____		
size: _____	Price $_____	Price $_____
toothpaste: brand _____		
size: _____	Price $_____	Price $_____
vitamin C: brand _____		
size: _____	Price $_____	Price $_____
dose: _____		
cough syrup: brand _____		
size: _____	Price $_____	Price $_____

97

JEWELRY STORE

1. bracelet
2. chain
3. diamond
4. emerald
5. engagement ring
6. jade
7. jeweler
8. necklace
9. pearl
10. pin
11. ring
12. ruby
13. turquoise
14. wedding ring/ wedding band
15. wristwatch
_____
_____

Group Role Play

Work in groups of three. • *Choose three people in the jewelry store.* • *Write a role play.* • *Include roles for everyone.* • *Present your role play to the class.*

Partner Interview

Partner's Name _____

Practice these questions with your teacher. • *Then ask your partner.*

1. Do you wear any jewelry? What do you wear?
2. What jewelry are you wearing today?
3. Do you ever buy jewelry? Who do you buy jewelry for?
4. Did you ever receive jewelry for a present? What did you get?

See Conversation Springboards on page 204.

HARDWARE STORE

1. bolts	9. handsaw	17. paintbrush	25. tape measure _____
2. chisel	10. hatchet	18. paint can	26. tool _____
3. crowbar	11. key	19. plane	27. tool box _____
4. duplicate	12. ladder	20. pliers	28. turpentine _____
5. electrical tape	13. level	21. power saw	29. vise _____
6. electric drill	14. lock	22. putty	30. washer _____
7. glue	15. nuts	23. sandpaper	31. wire
8. glue gun	16. paint	24. switch	32. wrench

Class Discussion

1. Do you ever go to the hardware store?
2. Which one?
3. What do you buy?
4. How are the prices?

Partner Activity

Partner's Name _____

Decide what is happening in the picture. • *Report your answers to the class.*

1. What is the man going to do with the ladder?
2. Why is the woman making a duplicate key?
3. What is the woman buying at the cash register?
4. What will the couple use the paint for? What color will they choose?

Class Game: *"Mime"*

Pantomime using a tool. • *Whoever guesses the tool takes the next turn.*

See Conversation Springboards on pages 204 and 205.

OFFICE SUPPLY STORE

1. binder
2. computer paper
3. correction fluid
4. desk calendar
5. envelope
6. file cabinet
7. greeting card
8. manila folder
9. masking tape
10. paper clip
11. rubber band
12. rubber cement
13. ruler
14. stapler
15. staples
16. tape
17. 3-hole punch
18. typewriter ribbon
19. typing paper

_____
_____
_____
_____
_____
_____

Class Discussion

What do you use these supplies for?

Find Someone Who

Review the vocabulary with your teacher. • *Fill in the name of someone who . . .*

1. _____ buys greeting cards.
2. _____ has a desk calendar.
3. _____ can type.
4. _____ wants to buy a file cabinet.
5. _____ can change a typewriter ribbon.

Group Activity

Work in groups of four or five. • *Put all your supplies on the desk.* • *Make a list of what your group has.* • *Compare your list with another group.*

See Conversation Springboards on page 205.

ELECTRONICS STORE

1. adding machine	9. computer keyboard	17. monitor	24. telephone jack
2. audiocassette	10. cordless phone	18. personal computer	25. turntable
3. black & white TV	11. electronic equipment	19. portable stereo	26. videotape
4. calculator	12. fax machine	system/boombox	_____
5. camcorder	13. floppy disk	20. printer	_____
6. car radio	14. headphones	21. shortwave radio	_____
7. color television	15. modem	22. tape deck	
8. compact disc (CD)	16. modular telephone	23. telephone cord	

Group Decision

Work in groups of five or six. • Decide on the best prices for the items in the picture. • Write prices on the tags. • Compare your prices with the class.

Class Discussion

1. What electronic equipment do you have? What do you want?
2. What electronic equipment do you like to use?
3. Do you use any of this equipment at work? What do you use?
4. What kind of electronic equipment is popular in your country? What do people have in their homes?

See Conversation Springboards on page 205.

SALES AND ADVERTISEMENTS

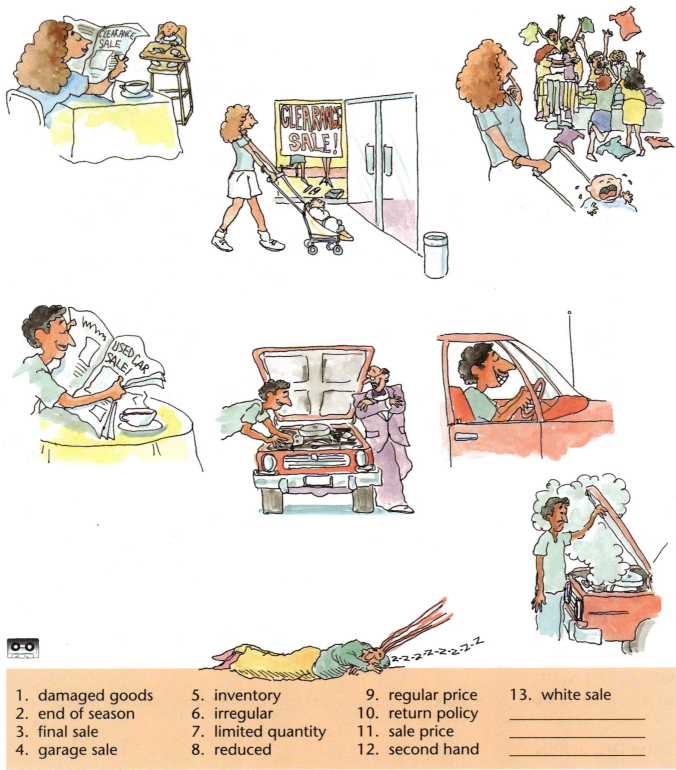

1. damaged goods	5. inventory	9. regular price	13. white sale
2. end of season	6. irregular	10. return policy	_____
3. final sale	7. limited quantity	11. sale price	_____
4. garage sale	8. reduced	12. second hand	_____

Strip Stories

Discuss these stories with your class. • *Did you ever have any of these experiences?* • *Tell the class.*

102   *See Conversation Springboards on page 205.*

Group Discussion

Work in groups of five. • *Discuss these questions.* • *Report your answers to the class.*

1. What kind of sales are these?
2. Do you like to shop at sales like these?
3. What have you bought on sale?
4. Is there a good sale now? Where?
5. What store in your community has the best sale?
6. Do you have to be careful when you buy on sale? Why or why not?

Community Activity

Bring in ads for sales to class. • *What do you want to buy?* • *How much money can you save?*

REVIEW

Group Decision

Work in groups of five. • *Your group has $1,000.* • *Decide how to spend it.* • *You can buy something together or divide the money.* • *If you divide it, each person decides how to spend his or her portion.* • *Report your decisions to the class.*

Remember to tell . . .

1. what you will buy.
2. where you will buy it.
3. who you will buy it for.
4. when you will buy it.
5. what you will do with it.

Partner Activity   Partner's Name _____

Ask your partner these questions. • *Then write a paragraph about your partner.* • *Read your paragraph to your partner.* • *Then read it to the class.*

1. Is money important to you? Why?
2. Do you ever save money?
3. What do you like to spend money on?
4. What don't you like to spend money on?
5. If you won the lottery, what would you do with the money?

Speech

Tell the class about your favorite store. • *Include everything you like about the store.* • *Show the class something you bought there.*

UNIT 7

COMMUNITY

LEARNING STRATEGIES

➤ Walk around your neighborhood. Make a list of everything you see. Then, in the Journal section of your notebook, describe your neighborhood. What different kinds of houses did you see? Focus on two or three people that you saw. Describe them.

➤ Find places in your community where you can speak English. Go there. Introduce yourself. Speak English!

YOUR NEIGHBORHOOD

1. apartment building	8. newsstand	15. shoemaker	22. trash can
2. building	9. parking meter	16. sidewalk	23. urban
3. convenience store	10. parking space	17. stickball	_____
4. crosswalk	11. pizza shop	18. stoop	_____
5. ice cream truck	12. playground	19. street corner	_____
6. laundromat	13. play in the street	20. traffic	_____
7. magazine store	14. recycling bin	21. traffic light	_____

See Conversation Springboards on page 205.

Class Discussion

1. Do you like your neighborhood? How long have you been living there?
2. Is there a traffic light on your street? Where is it?
3. Does the ice cream truck come to your neighborhood? When?
4. Do children play in the street in your neighborhood? What do they play?
5. Where do people walk their dogs in your neighborhood?

Find Someone Who

Review the vocabulary with your teacher. • *Fill in the name of someone who . . .*

1. _____ lives in an apartment building.
2. _____ shops in a convenience store.
3. _____ recycles cans and bottles.
4. _____ lives near a playground.
5. _____ likes to play stickball.

YOUR COMMUNITY

1. across from
2. around the corner
3. bank
4. behind
5. between
6. bus
7. church
8. hospital
9. in front of
10. just before
11. just past
12. library
13. movie theater
14. next to
15. on the corner
16. opposite
17. parking lot
18. post office
19. public phone
20. school
21. straight ahead
22. subway
23. taxi
24. train
25. turn right/left
26. (two) blocks

See Conversation Springboards on page 206.

Class Discussion

1. Does your community look like this? What buildings do you recognize?
2. Do you go to the library? Does the library have a foreign book section? What languages? Do you have a library card?
3. When do you go to the post office? What do you ask for? Do you ever have problems there?
4. Is there a bank in your community? Do you use it? When? What do you do there?
5. Is there public transportation in your community? Is it good? Do you use it? When do you use it?

Partner Role Play   Partner's Name _____

Complete these conversations. • *Use the picture on page 108.* • *Present your conversations to the class.*

1. **at the hospital**
   A: Excuse me. How can I get to the post office?
   B: _____
   A: Thank you.

2. **at the bank**
   A: Excuse me. Can you tell me how to get to the library?
   B: _____
   A: Thanks.

3. **at the movie theater**
   A: Pardon me. Could you please tell me where I can park my car?
   B: _____
   A: Thanks very much.

4. **at the library**
   A: Pardon me. Do you know where I can make a phone call?
   B: _____
   A: Thanks a lot.

5. **at the subway station**
   A: Say, can you tell me where the school is?
   B: _____
   A: Thank you.

THE TELEPHONE

1. answering machine	7. hold	13. telephone call	_____
2. busy signal	8. local call	14. telephone number	_____
3. cord	9. long distance	15. touch tone	_____
4. cordless	10. message	16. wrong number	_____
5. directory assistance	11. operator		_____
6. hang up	12. receiver		_____

Class Discussion

What is happening in these pictures?

Partner Interview

Partner's Name _____

Practice these questions with your teacher. • *Then ask your partner.*

1. What is your telephone number?
2. What is your area code?
3. What kind of telephone do you have?

4. Do you make a lot of long distance calls? Where do you call?
5. Who do you call most often?

Cross-Cultural Exchange

What are telephones like in your country? • *How do you make a long distance call?* • *Do many people have telephones in their homes?*

110

See Conversation Springboards on page 206.

Partner Role Play

Partner's Name _____

Complete these phone conversations. • *Present one to the class.*

1. **answering machine**

   Machine: I'm not here right now. Please leave a message at the tone. BEEEEEP!

   You: _____

2. **leaving a message**

   Stranger: Hello.

   You: Hello. May I please speak to _____?

   Stranger: S/he's not home. May I take a message?

   You: Yes. _____. My telephone

   number is _____.

3. **wrong number**

   Stranger: Hello.

   You: Hello. This is _____. Is _____ there?

   Stranger: _____

   You: _____

Partner Role Play

Partner's Name _____

Decide what to say for these phone calls. • *Present one conversation to the class.*

1. local directory assistance for the number of your school
2. your school when you can't come to class
3. the landlord when your roof is leaking
4. the pharmacy when you need to know their hours
5. the telephone company when your bill is incorrect

Community Activity

Use your local telephone directory. • *Find the names, addresses, and telephone numbers.*

LOOK UP	NAME	ADDRESS	TELEPHONE NUMBER
1. a pharmacy	_____	_____	_____
2. a movie theater	_____	_____	_____
3. a restaurant	_____	_____	_____
4. a plumber	_____	_____	_____
5. a church	_____	_____	_____
6. your school	_____	_____	_____
7. your hospital	_____	_____	_____
8. the telephone company business office	_____	_____
9. local directory assistance	_____	_____
10. long distance directory assistance	_____	_____

EMERGENCY: FIRE!

1. ambulance	5. fire escape	10. hose	15. stretcher
2. ax	6. fire fighter	11. put out a fire	16. victim
3. burn	7. fire hydrant	12. rescue	_____
4. Emergency Medical Technician (EMT)	8. flame	13. siren	_____
	9. hook	14. smoke	_____

Class Discussion

What is happening? • What do you think caused the fire? • How can fires be prevented?

See Conversation Springboards on page 206.

What's the Story?

Work in groups of four. • *Choose one person in the picture.* • *Tell that person's story.* •
Everyone in the group should contribute at least one sentence. • *Read your story to the class.*

1. What is his/her name?
2. Why is he/she at the fire scene?
3. What is he/she doing?
4. What will happen next?

Group Discussion

Work in groups of four. • *Discuss these questions.* • *Report your answers to the class.*

1. Have you ever seen a fire? What happened?
2. Are you afraid of fire? Why or why not?
3. Did you play with fire when you were a child? If so, what did you do?
4. Are fires a problem in your country? Why or why not?
5. Tell the most interesting story to the class.

Partner Role Play   Partner's Name _____

Write a conversation to report a fire to the 911 emergency operator. • *Present your conversation
to the class.*

911 Operator: _____

You: _____

911 Operator: _____

You: _____

911 Operator: _____

You: _____

EMERGENCY: POLICE!

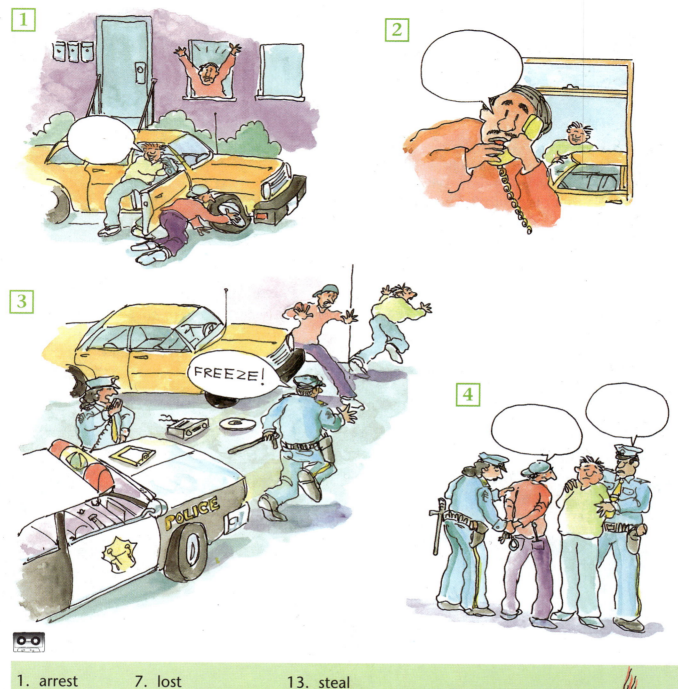

1. arrest
2. break in
3. crash
4. crime
5. danger
6. handcuffs
7. lost
8. Miranda rights
9. owner
10. police car
11. police report
12. report a crime
13. steal _____
14. surrender/give up _____
15. thief _____
16. walkie-talkie _____
17. witness _____

Strip Story

What is happening? • *Fill in the bubbles.* • *Discuss this story with your class.*

See Conversation Springboards on pages 206 and 207.

Group Decision

Work in groups of four. • *What should you do in these emergencies?* • *Decide with your group.* • *Report your decisions to the class.*

Partner Activity

Partner's Name _____

Choose one emergency. • *Write a conversation between the 911 operator and yourself.* • *Present your conversation to the class.*

1. Who are you?
2. Where are you?
3. What happened?
4. When did it happen?
5. Is anyone hurt?
6. What should you do while you wait?

THE POST OFFICE

1. air mail	8. mailbox	14. postal clerk
2. book of stamps	9. mail carrier/	15. postal worker
3. first class	letter carrier	16. scale
4. insurance	10. mail truck	17. stamp
5. letter	11. overnight mail	18. stamp machine
6. mail	12. parcel post	19. third class
7. mail bag	13. postage	20. two-day delivery

Class Discussion

What is happening in the picture?

Class Game: "What do you remember?"

Look at the picture. • Remember as much as you can. • Close your book. • List everything. • Compare your answers with your class. • Who had the longest list? • Open your book and check your answers.

See Conversation Springboards on page 207.

Partner Activity

Choose a person who is waiting in line in the picture. • *Write a paragraph about that person and read it to the class.*

1. What is the person's name?
2. What is he/she doing at the post office?
3. What will he/she say when it is his/her turn?
4. Where is the letter or package going?
5. Who will receive it?

Partner Role Play

Write a conversation for you and a postal clerk. • *Present your conversation to the class.*

1. What do you want at the post office?
2. What will the clerk say to you?
3. What will you say to the clerk?
4. How much money will you need?

Partner Interview

Practice these questions with your teacher. • *Then ask your partner.*

1. Do you like to write letters?
2. How often do you write letters?
3. Who do you write to?
4. How often do you receive letters?
5. How often do you go to the post office?
6. What do you do there?

Group Problem Posing/Problem Solving

Work in groups of three. • *State the problem.* • *Find a solution.* • *Report your decisions to the class.*

You wait in line for ten minutes at the post office. You buy a book of stamps and send two letters air mail. It costs you $9.30. You give the clerk a $50.00 bill. The clerk gives you $10.70 in change.

THE BANK

1. account
2. automated teller machine (ATM)
3. bankbook
4. bank officer
5. cash
6. cash a check
7. checking account
8. credit card
9. deposit slip
10. loan application
11. money order
12. monthly statement
13. overdraw
14. personal check
15. personal identification number (PIN)
16. safety deposit box
17. save
18. savings account
19. teller
20. traveler's check
21. withdrawal slip
_____
_____
_____
_____

Class Activity

What are the people doing in the bank? • *Make a list on the board of everything they are doing.*

Class Discussion

1. What is the name of the bank closest to your home? Where is it?
2. Do you use the bank?
3. When do you go to the bank?
4. Do you have a savings account? a checking account?
5. What are some things you can put in a safety deposit box?

See Conversation Springboards on page 207.

Group Problem Posing/Problem Solving

Work in groups of three. • State the problems. • Find solutions. • Report your decisions to the class. • Present a role play about one of these problems.

This woman works in a bank. She's a teller. You are cashing a check for $50, and she gives you $60. What do you say? What will she do?

This man is robbing the bank. What will the teller do? What will the robber do? What would you do if you were there?

This man overdrew his account. What will he do? What should you do if you overdraw your account?

PUBLIC TRANSPORTATION

1. bus driver	7. exit	13. metro	19. subway station	24. wait in line
2. bus stop	8. fare	14. passenger	20. taxi driver	_____
3. cab	9. front	15. platform	21. token booth	_____
4. engineer	10. front door	16. rear	22. transfer	
5. entrance	11. get off	17. rear door	23. turnstile	
6. exact change	12. get on	18. seat		

Class Discussion

1. What kind of public transportation do you have in your community?
2. Do you use it? When?
3. How much is the bus fare? the subway fare?
4. Is it crowded? When is it most crowded?
5. Do you get on at the front or at the rear of the bus/train? Where do you get off?
6. What do you say if you want to get off?
7. Is it safe to ride on public transportation? dangerous? When is it dangerous? Why is it dangerous?

See Conversation Springboards on pages 207 and 208.

Group Role Play

Work in groups of three. • *Write a role play between the taxi driver and the two passengers.* • *Include roles for everyone.* • *Present your role play to the class.*

Group Problem Posing/Problem Solving

Work in groups of three. • *State the problems.* • *Find solutions.* • *Report your decisions to the class.*
1. You take the bus to school on the first day of class. After two stops, you realize you are on the wrong bus.
2. You are in a subway station with two friends, waiting for the train. The train comes. You get on, but the door closes too fast. Your friends are still on the station platform.
3. You get on the bus. After the bus starts, you realize you don't have exact change.

Group Survey

Ask everyone in your group these questions. • *Check the kinds of transportation and their advantages.* • *Count your answers.* • *Report your group's results to the class.* • *Write the class' results on the board.*

	ADVANTAGES			
What are the advantages of using . . .	cheap	convenient	fast	safe
1. the bus?	_____	_____	_____	_____
2. the train?	_____	_____	_____	_____
3. a taxi?	_____	_____	_____	_____
4. a private car?	_____	_____	_____	_____
5. a bicycle?	_____	_____	_____	_____
6. your feet?	_____	_____	_____	_____

YOUR CAR

1. accelerator (gas pedal)
2. automatic (shift)
3. baby seat
4. brake
5. bumper
6. car key
7. clutch
8. convertible
9. emergency brake
10. exhaust pipe
11. fender
12. fuel gauge
13. gas cap

14. gear shift
15. glove compartment
16. headlight
17. hood
18. hubcap
19. ignition
20. license plate
21. rear view mirror
22. seat belt
23. signal light
24. speedometer
25. standard (shift)
26. steering wheel

27. tachometer
28. tail light
29. temperature gauge
30. trunk
31. visor
32. wheel
33. windshield
34. windshield wiper
_____
_____
_____
_____

Partner Interview

Partner's Name _____

Practice these questions with your teacher. • *Then ask your partner.*

1. Do you have a driver's license?
2. Do you have a car? What kind?
3. Do you drive a standard shift? an automatic?
4. What kind of car would you like to drive?
5. What is the most popular car in your country?

See Conversation Springboards on page 208.

TRAFFIC AND ROAD SIGNS

Class Discussion

1. Have you ever seen any of these signs? Which ones?
2. What should you do . . .
   at a Railroad Crossing sign?
   at a Yield sign?
   at a Speed Limit sign?
   at a School Zone sign?

Community Activity

Which of these signs is in your neighborhood? • What color is each sign? • Draw the signs in your neighborhood. • Note the colors. • Bring your signs to class. • What do they say? • What do the colors signify?

See Conversation Springboards on page 208.

THE GAS STATION

1. air	7. gas pump	13. radiator _____
2. attendant	8. inspection	14. repairs _____
3. engine	9. lever	15. self-service _____
4. full service	10. lift	16. tire _____
5. gallon	11. oil	17. unleaded _____
6. gas/gasoline	12. premium (high-test)	_____

Partner Activity

Partner's Name _____

Decide what to say. • Present your conversations to the class.

1. You want the attendant to check your oil.
2. You want $10 worth of super unleaded gasoline.
3. You have a flat tire and need some help.
4. You need your car inspected.

Group Vocabulary Challenge

Work in groups of four or five. • Make a list of vocabulary words about cars and gas stations. • Compare your list with another group. • Which group had the most new words? • Make a list on the board. • Copy the new words into your notebook.

124   *See Conversation Springboards on page 208.*

THE LAUNDROMAT AND DRY CLEANERS

1. bleach	7. dry-clean	13. rinse cycle	19. wash cycle
2. clean	8. hanger	14. sort	20. white wash
3. cold water	9. hot water	15. spin cycle	_____
4. dark wash	10. laundry basket	16. spot	_____
5. detergent	11. load	17. starch	_____
6. dirty	12. press	18. warm water	_____

Partner Game: *"What do you remember?"*   Partner's Name _____

Look at the picture with your partner. • Remember as much as you can. • Close your book. • Describe the picture with your partner. • List everything. • Compare your list with another pair. • Add to your list.

What's the Story?

Work in groups of five. • Write a story about the scene in the laundromat. • Everyone in the group should contribute at least two sentences. • Use these questions or make up your own. • Read your story to the class.

1. Who are the people?
2. What are their names?
3. What day is it?
4. What time is it?

See Conversation Springboards on page 208.

REVIEW

Speech

Choose a topic and explain it to the class.

1. How do you use public transportation?
2. How do you get gas at a self-service station?
3. How do you wash clothes at the laundromat?
4. How do you call directory assistance?
5. How do you buy stamps at the post office?
6. How do you report a fire emergency?

Partner Vocabulary Challenge   Partner's Name _____

Make lists to answer each question. • Read your lists to the class.

1. What do people do at the bank?
2. What do people do at the post office?
3. What emergencies do people call 911 for?
4. What do people do at the gas station?
5. What do people do at the dry cleaners?

Community Activity

Draw a map from your school to your house. • Explain your map to the class.

WORK

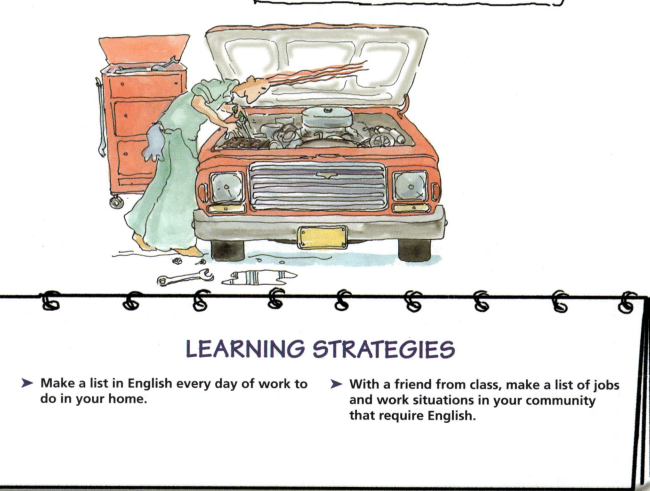

LEARNING STRATEGIES

➤ Make a list in English every day of work to do in your home.

➤ With a friend from class, make a list of jobs and work situations in your community that require English.

WORK EVERYONE DOES!

1. change a light bulb	7. dust/polish the furniture	13. rake the leaves
2. clean the refrigerator	8. feed the dog	14. vacuum the carpet/rug
3. cook a meal	9. fold the clothes	15. wash the windows
4. defrost the freezer	10. hammer a nail	_____
5. do housework	11. hang a picture	_____
6. dry the dishes	12. iron the clothes	_____

Group Survey

Ask everyone in your group these questions. • *Check EVERY DAY, OFTEN, OCCASIONALLY, or NEVER.* • *Count your answers.* • *Report your group's results to the class.* • *Write the class' results on the board.*

How often do you . . .	EVERY DAY	OFTEN	OCCASIONALLY	NEVER
1. cook?	_____	_____	_____	_____
2. change a light bulb?	_____	_____	_____	_____
3. wash the dishes?	_____	_____	_____	_____
4. hammer a nail?	_____	_____	_____	_____
5. paint the house?	_____	_____	_____	_____
6. dust the furniture?	_____	_____	_____	_____
7. rake the leaves?	_____	_____	_____	_____

See Conversation Springboards on pages 208 and 209.

Class Game: *"Test Your Memory"*

Close your book. • *Listen to your teacher tell the story about the family in the pictures.* • *Open your book.* • *Write the correct order in the boxes.* • *Read your story to the class in the correct order.*

Cross-Cultural Exchange

Who does the housework in your home? • *Should men help with the housework?* • *In your country, do men help with the housework?* • *Why or why not?* • *What electrical appliances do people use to do housework in your country?*

HOME REPAIRS

1. battery	7. material/cloth	13. screwdriver
2. board (wood)	8. needle	14. sew
3. circuit breaker	9. putty knife	15. sewing machine
4. flashlight	10. saw	16. spool of thread
5. flip a switch	11. scissors	
6. hinge	12. screw	

Class Activity

Make a list on the board of what home repairs these people are making. • What tools are they using? • Copy the list into your notebook.

Group Decision

Work in groups of five. • Decide what to do for each situation. • Report your decisions to the class.

1. The sink is clogged in the bathroom.
2. Your daughter dropped her gold ring down the toilet.
3. The lights went out in the house.
4. There is a small hole in the wall of the living room.
5. A shelf fell off the wall.

130

See Conversation Springboards on page 209.

What's the Story?

Work in groups of five. • *Choose one of the pictures and write a story.* • *Everyone in the group should contribute at least two sentences.* • *Read your story to the class.*

Answer these questions:
1. Who?
2. What?
3. Where?
4. When?
5. Why?

Find Someone Who

Review the vocabulary with your teacher. • *Fill in the name of someone who . . .*
1. _____ knows how to sew.
2. _____ has a flashlight.
3. _____ can use a saw.
4. _____ makes repairs at home.
5. _____ owns a sewing machine.

JOBS

1. barber	7. farm worker	12. manicurist _____
2. carpenter	8. fisherman	13. mechanic _____
3. chef	9. full-time	14. part-time _____
4. construction worker	10. hospital aide	15. secretary _____
5. engineer	11. mailman/	16. security guard _____
6. factory worker	mail carrier	17. teacher aide _____

Class Discussion

Where do these people work? • What do they do?

Group Activity

Work in groups of five. • Fill in the chart with your group. • Compare your answers with another group. • Report your answers to the class.

WHO?	WHAT?	WHERE?
1. farm worker	picks crops	on a farm
2. teacher	teaches	in a school
3. factory worker		
4. cook		
5. manicurist		
6. secretary		
7. barber		
8. hospital aide		
9. mechanic		
10. salesperson		
11. security guard		
12. taxi driver		

132   *See Conversation Springboards on page 209.*

Group Activity

Work in groups of five. • *Decide with your group what jobs these people have.* • *For number five, decide on a job.* • *Draw a picture.* • *Write the job title.* • *Report your decision to the class.*

1._____   2._____   5._____

3._____   4._____

Partner Role Play

Partner's Name _____

A TV host is interviewing you. • *Choose a job.* • *Write a conversation between the TV host and yourself.* • *Present your role play to the class.*

1. Where do you work?
2. What is your job?
3. What hours do you work?

4. Do you like your job?
5. What job do you want in the future?

CLOTHING FOR WORK

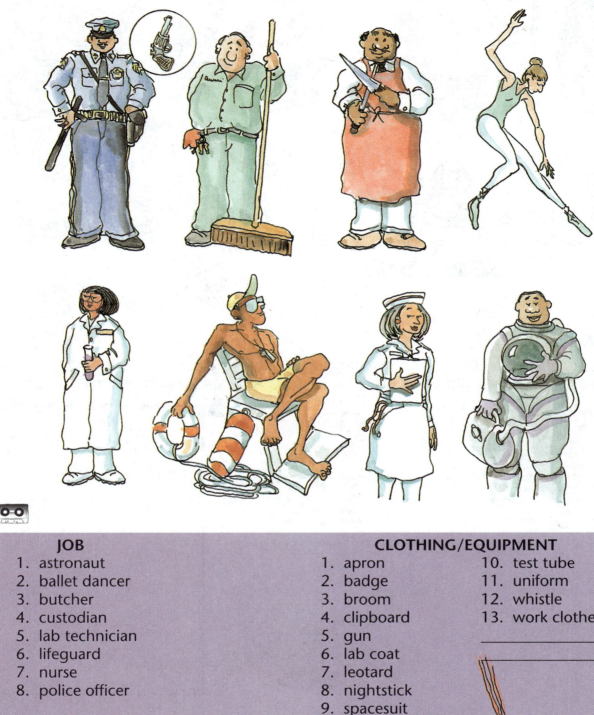

JOB	CLOTHING/EQUIPMENT	
1. astronaut	1. apron	10. test tube
2. ballet dancer	2. badge	11. uniform
3. butcher	3. broom	12. whistle
4. custodian	4. clipboard	13. work clothes
5. lab technician	5. gun	_____
6. lifeguard	6. lab coat	_____
7. nurse	7. leotard	
8. police officer	8. nightstick	
	9. spacesuit	

Class Discussion

1. What work do these people do?
2. Why do they wear uniforms or costumes?
3. Who pays for the uniforms?
4. Which uniforms do you like? Why?
5. Which uniforms require special shoes? special hats? special gloves?

See Conversation Springboards on page 209.

Group Discussion

Work in groups of four. • *Look at the pictures.* • *Discuss these questions.* • *Report your opinions to the class.*

1. What are the people wearing?
2. What are their jobs?

3. Are they dressed appropriately?
4. What do you wear to work?

Cross-Cultural Exchange

In your country, do work clothes look like this? • *Which are the same?* • *Which are different?*

SAFETY AT WORK

1. assembly line	5. mask	9. safety violation	_____
2. co-worker	6. plant	10. signs	_____
3. foreman	7. safety gloves	11. steel-tipped shoes	_____
4. machine	8. safety goggles	12. supervisor	_____

Class Discussion

1. What is happening in this picture?
2. What jobs do these people have?
3. Do you think anyone is a supervisor? Which one(s)?
4. Are there any safety violations in the factory? What are the violations?
5. What kind of factory do you think it is?

Group Decision

Work in groups of five. • Decide what the people are saying. • Fill in the bubbles. • Compare your bubbles with the class.

See Conversation Springboards on page 210.

Class Discussion

What do these signs mean? • Where do you see these signs?

Group Role Play

Work in groups of four or five. • Choose one of these situations. • Write a role play. • Include roles for everyone. • Present your role play to the class.

1. You are new on the job. You are unsure of what to do. Ask your co-workers. When no one knows for sure, check with your supervisor.
2. It's Friday afternoon. You are taking a break. Several co-workers are sitting in the lounge having coffee and snacks. Have a conversation.

Community Activity

Are there any signs in the school building? • What do they say? • Do you notice any signs at your job? • Copy them and bring them to class. • Look for signs in other buildings. • Copy the signs. • Show the signs to the class. • Who can guess where the sign is from?

WORKING ON A FARM

1. barn	6. chick	11. ewe	16. lamb	21. rooster _____
2. barnyard	7. corral	12. foal	17. mare	22. sheep _____
3. boar	8. cow	13. goose	18. pig	23. silo _____
4. bull	9. duck	14. gosling	19. piglet	24. sow _____
5. calf	10. duckling	15. hen	20. ram	25. stallion _____

Cross-Cultural Exchange

What do these animals "say" in your native language? • *Fill in the chart.*

ANIMAL	ENGLISH SOUND	YOUR LANGUAGE
1. cat	meow	_____
2. dog	bow wow	_____
3. cow	moo	_____
4. rooster	cock-a-doodle-doo	_____
5. hen	cluck-cluck	_____
6. horse	neigh	_____
7. pig	oink	_____
8. duck	quack	_____

See Conversation Springboards on page 210.

1. bucket	6. hay	11. pitchfork	16. trough
2. clippers	7. milk a cow	12. plow a field	17. wool
3. feed bag	8. milking machine	13. rope	_____
4. field	9. orchard	14. shear a sheep	_____
5. harvest corn	10. pick apples	15. tractor	_____

Class Discussion

What is happening in these pictures? • What other work do people do on farms and ranches?

Find Someone Who

Review the vocabulary with your teacher. • Fill in the name of someone who . . .

1. _____ loves horses.
2. _____ has visited or lived on a farm.
3. _____ has picked fruit.
4. _____ can make animal sounds.

See Conversation Springboards on page 210.

PROBLEMS AT WORK

1. appropriate behavior
2. boss
3. company time
4. discrimination
5. employee
6. employer
7. excuse
8. late
9. lazy
10. personal problem
11. rude
12. (sexual) harassment
13. understanding
_____
_____

Class Discussion

What is happening in each of these pictures? • Discuss the problems together.

See Conversation Springboards on page 210.

Group Problem Posing/Problem Solving

Work in groups of four. • *State the problems in the pictures.* • *Pick one problem.* • *Find a solution.* • *Role-play the problem and the solution for the class.*

Conversation Squares

Work in groups of three. • *First write your own answers.* • *Then ask your partners the questions.* • *Write their answers.* • *Compare your group's answers with other groups.*

Problem at Work	You _____	Partner 1 _____	Partner 2 _____
1. What was it?	_____	_____	_____
2. How long did it last?	_____	_____	_____
3. What was the solution?	_____	_____	_____
4. Who helped you?	_____	_____	_____

LOSING YOUR JOB

1. close down	5. migrant work	9. seasonal work
2. fire	6. out of work	10. slow down
3. lay off	7. poor performance	11. temporary
4. manager	8. quit	12. unemployed

_____
_____
_____
_____

Strip Stories

Discuss these stories with the class. • *Decide what is happening.* • *Write captions.*

Find Someone Who

Review the vocabulary with your teacher. • *Fill in the name of someone who . . .*

1. _____ has been laid off.
2. _____ has quit a job.
3. _____ has kept a bad job.
4. _____ has left a good job.
5. _____ has had seasonal work.

See Conversation Springboards on pages 210 and 211.

_____ _____ _____

_____ _____ _____

Group Activity

Work in groups of three. • _Answer these questions._ • _Compare your answers with others in the class._

1. What are good reasons to quit a job?

_____
_____
_____
_____

2. What are good reasons to keep a job?

_____
_____
_____
_____

3. What are good reasons to fire an employee?

_____
_____
_____
_____

FINDING A JOB

WANT ADS

TRUCK LOADER
Moving truck loader. P/T work; will turn into F/T for right person. Willing to work all 3 shifts. This person should be strong, not afraid to work. Salary based on performance. APPLY AT CASA-WORKS FURNITURE, 3945 S. Main St., across from post office.

SECURITY OFFICERS
F/T or P/T, exp. preferred but not mandatory. Will train. Progressive wages. Must be 21 or older, have home telephone and reliable transportation. Apply in person at SECURITY SERVICES, 4455 S. Park Avenue, 555-3056. Women encouraged to apply. $200/week.

COURIER
For busy route. Los Angeles area. Good driving record a must. Mon.–Fri. $8/hr. Call Pat, 555-4956.

COUNTER POSITION
Part time. Apply in person at DayTime Dry Cleaners. 354 River St.

LA CASITA
Seeking qualified individuals for the following positions:
HOUSEKEEPERS
We offer:
• health benefits
• paid time off
• mileage incentive program
Please apply in person:
La Casita Hotel
3 Casita Drive
Pleasant Valley
555-3956. EOE

DENTAL RECEPTIONIST
Bilingual; work w/great team. P/T, 1:30-6:30 p.m., Mon.–Fri., some Sat. Will train. Mature person w/good people skills. Apply 345 Rosewood. $15,000

NURSE ASSISTANTS
A BRIGHT FUTURE WAITS FOR YOU! Health Care Associates has staffing opportunities for Nurse Assistants. Put your valuable skills to work in area hospitals and nursing homes. Health Care Associates offers:
• a chance to design a work schedule that works for you
• competitive salary

• the support of a highly respected, professional organization
Call Jill for more information, 555-5676.

BRIGHTEN YOUR FUTURE WITH HEALTH CARE!
Adult Care Home needs responsible, experienced people for all shifts. Must have own transportation. Call 555-3455.

WE CARE CAR WASH
Needs full-time and part-time help. Apply in person. 240th and B'way.

DIRECTOR OF PUBLIC RELATIONS WANTED
Resp. incl. promotional & community relations efforts. College or graduate degree in Public Relations and/or work exp. in field. Strong written & verbal communications skills. Eng/Span speaker desirable. Up to $30,000. For complete description, call Maria: 555-3029 or mail resume to:
MUSEUM OF INTERNATIONAL ARTS, 245 Grand Ave., Tucson, AZ 85611.

CASHIER
Permanent position. Pharmacy experience pref. Must be reliable. Benefits. Will consider college students. Call 555-0034.

SCHOOLS & INSTRUCTION

BANK TRAINING
in 4 to 8 weeks. Accredited Member NATTS. Financial aid if qualified. Job placement assistance. Day or evening classes. Call 555-5678.

BE A DOG GROOMER!
18-week course! Hands-on training. Financial aid if qualified. Call now for information: 555-6554, Pedigree Career Institute.

GET A CAREER IN GEAR!
Auto/Diesel Technology Associate Degree Program. Financial Aid Assistance if qualified. ADC Technical and Trade School, 12 Technical Drive, 555-2345.

Class Discussion

1. Where do you think these ads are from? Have you ever seen ads like these?
2. Did you ever apply for a job through a newspaper ad? When? What kind of job was it?
3. What information do you look for in an ad?
4. When do you apply for a job through an ad?
5. Which one of these jobs in the newspaper ads interests you? Why?

See Conversation Springboards on page 211.

Write

Fill out this employment application. • Use it in the role play below.

Date: _____   _____   _____
    (Month)   (Day)   (Year)

Name: _____
    (First)   (Middle Initial)   (Last)

Social Security Number: _____

Address: _____
    (Number)   (Street)   (Apartment)

_____
    (City)   (State)   (ZIP Code)

Telephone: _(____)_____
    (Area Code)

Job Applying for: _____

Work Experience: _____

_____

_____

_____

Education: _____

_____

_____

_____

Partner Role Play

Partner's Name _____

Choose a job from the ads. • One partner is the applicant. • One is the interviewer. • Present your conversation to the class.

Applicant: *Ask some of these questions (or others):*
1. "What are the responsibilities of the job?"
2. "What are the hours?"
3. "Do I have to wear a uniform? Does the company provide the uniform?"
4. "What is the salary?"
5. "What are the company benefits? What am I eligible for?"

Interviewer: *Ask some of these questions (or others):*
1. "Why are you interested in this job?"
2. "Why are you thinking of leaving your present job?"
3. "Do you have any experience for this job?"
4. "Can you read and write English?"
5. "Can you work overtime?"

BENEFITS

1. deduct
2. disability
3. family leave
4. health insurance
5. hospitalization
6. paid holiday
7. pension
8. retirement
9. sick day
10. unemployment
11. vacation
12. workers' compensation

_____
_____
_____
_____
_____
_____

Class Discussion

Which of these benefits is most important to you? • Which benefits do you have in your present job?

146

See Conversation Springboards on page 211.

Group Discussion

Work in groups of five or six. • *Discuss these questions.* • *Report your answers to the class.*
1. When do you take a sick day?
2. What do you do on your vacation?
3. What days are paid holidays?
4. When do you get hospital benefits?
5. What do you want to do when you retire?
6. What is "family leave"?
7. When does a worker qualify for workers' compensation?

Group Vocabulary Challenge

Work in groups of five or six. • *Make a list of the reasons to take a sick day.* • *Read your list to the class.* • *Which group had the most new words?* • *Make a list on the board.* • *Copy the new words into your notebook.*

Class Game: *"What do you want to do on your next vacation?"*

Think. • *Write.* • *Fold.* • *Make a pile of papers.* • *Choose one.* • *Guess who wrote it.*

Group Problem Posing/Problem Solving

Work in groups of five or six. • *State this man's problem in one or two sentences.* • *Find a solution.* • *Compare your decisions with another group.*

Cross-Cultural Exchange

What benefits do employees usually get in your country? • *What is deducted from employees' paychecks?*

REVIEW

Partner Interview

Partner's Name _____

Practice these questions with your teacher. • *Then ask your partner.*

1. Where do you work?
2. What is your job?
3. What do you wear to work?
4. Do you work part time or full time?
5. When do you work?

6. Do you like your job?
7. Why or why not?
8. What is your boss like?
9. What do you want to do in the future?

Write

Write about your job.

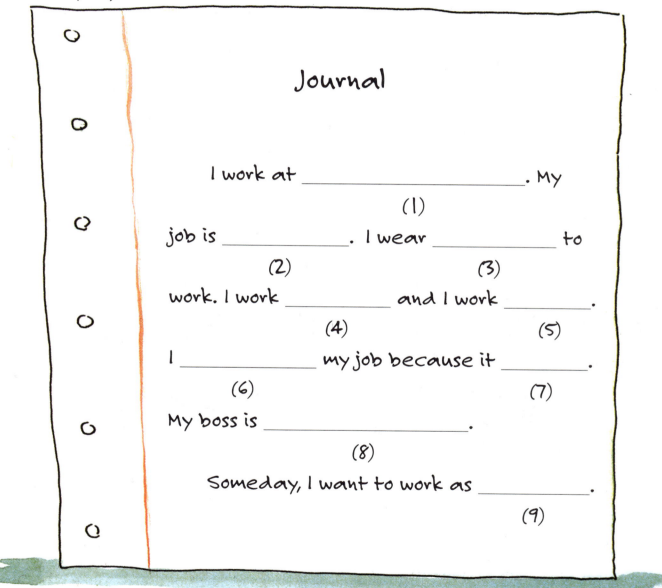

Journal

I work at _____. My
(1)

job is _____. I wear _____ to
(2)   (3)

work. I work _____ and I work _____.
(4)   (5)

I _____ my job because it _____.
(6)   (7)

My boss is _____.
(8)

Someday, I want to work as _____.
(9)

Tell Your Partner

Read your journal entry to your partner. • *Listen to your partner's journal.*

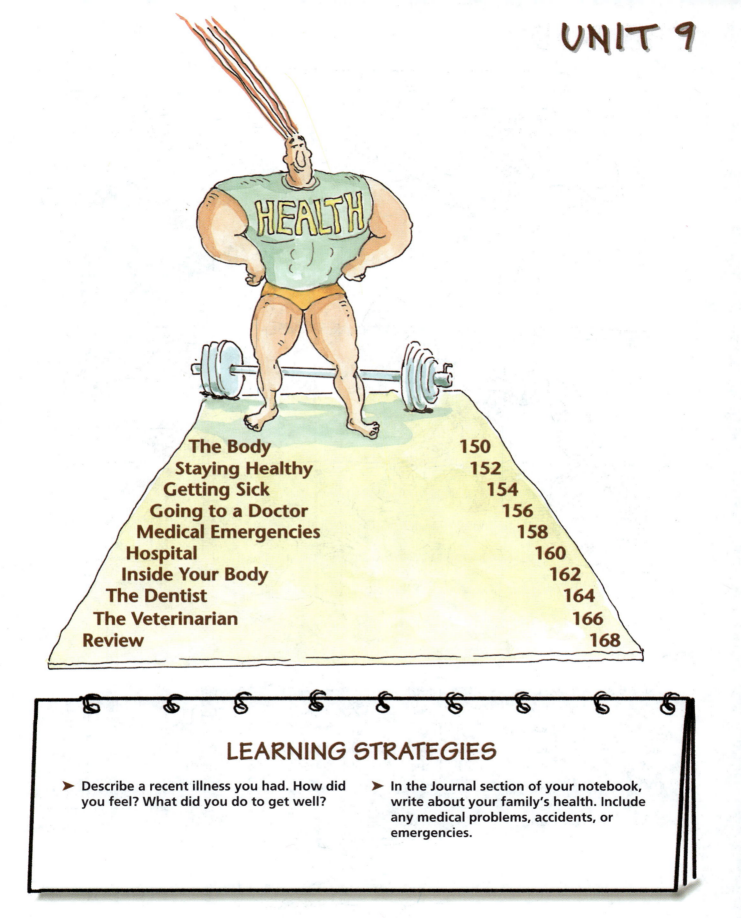

HEALTH

LEARNING STRATEGIES

➤ Describe a recent illness you had. How did you feel? What did you do to get well?

➤ In the Journal section of your notebook, write about your family's health. Include any medical problems, accidents, or emergencies.

THE BODY

1. ankle	9. ear	17. head	25. neck	30. thigh
2. arm	10. elbow	18. heel	26. nose	31. thumb
3. back	11. exercise	19. hip	27. shin	32. toe
4. buttocks	12. face	20. jaw	28. shoulder	33. toenail
5. calf	13. finger	21. knee	29. sweat	34. tooth
6. cheek	14. fingernail	22. leg		35. waist
7. chest	15. forehead	23. lip		36. work out
8. chin	16. hand	24. mouth		37. wrist

See Conversation Springboards on pages 211 and 212.

Group Game: *"What is it?"*

Work in groups of six. • Choose a leader.

  Leader: *Think about a part of the body. • Don't say what it is.*
  Group: *Ask the leader YES/NO questions.*
  Leader: *Answer "Yes" or "No."*
  Group: *Try to guess the word. Whoever guesses is the new leader.*

Class Game: *"Follow the Leader"*

Practice these instructions with your teacher. • Close your book. • Listen to your teacher. •
Follow the instructions.

1. Stand up.
2. Nod your head ("yes").
3. Shake your head ("no").
4. Raise your left hand.
5. Touch your toes.
6. Put your hands on your hips.
7. Bend to the right.
8. Sit down.

STAYING HEALTHY

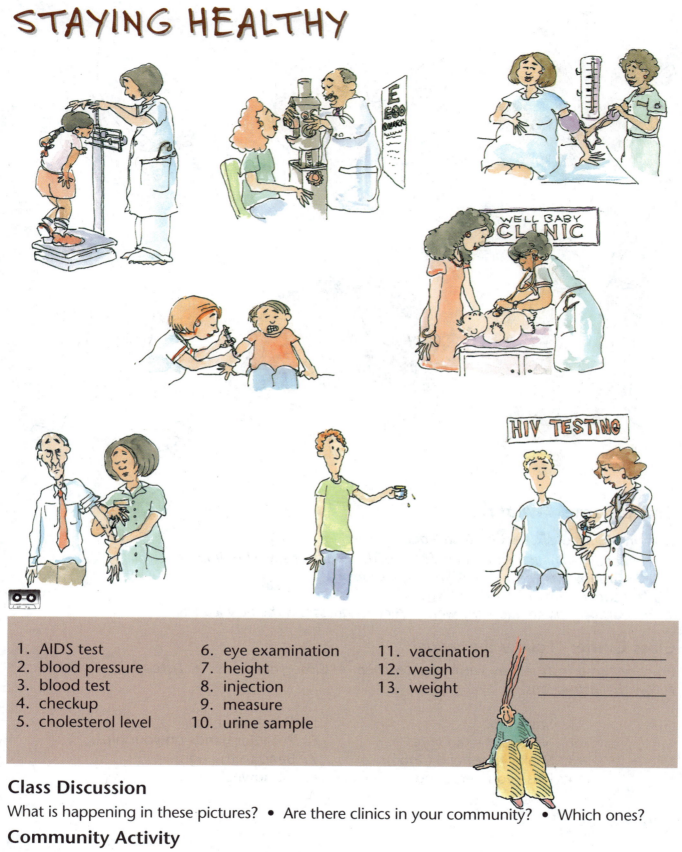

1. AIDS test
2. blood pressure
3. blood test
4. checkup
5. cholesterol level
6. eye examination
7. height
8. injection
9. measure
10. urine sample
11. vaccination
12. weigh
13. weight
_____
_____
_____

Class Discussion

What is happening in these pictures? • Are there clinics in your community? • Which ones?

Community Activity

Look in the telephone directory for the number of the Board of Health or your community hospital. • On the board list questions you want to ask. • Call the number to find the answers.

See Conversation Springboards on page 212.

Group Activity

Work in groups of five. • *How can you stay healthy?* • *Everyone in the group should contribute one answer to each question.* • *Compare your answers with the rest of the class.*

What is a healthy meal?

Student's Name	Advice
1. _____	
2. _____	
3. _____	
4. _____	
5. _____	

What is the best kind of exercise?

Student's Name	Advice
1. _____	
2. _____	
3. _____	
4. _____	
5. _____	

How many hours of sleep do you need each night?

Student's Name	Advice
1. _____	
2. _____	
3. _____	
4. _____	
5. _____	

GETTING SICK

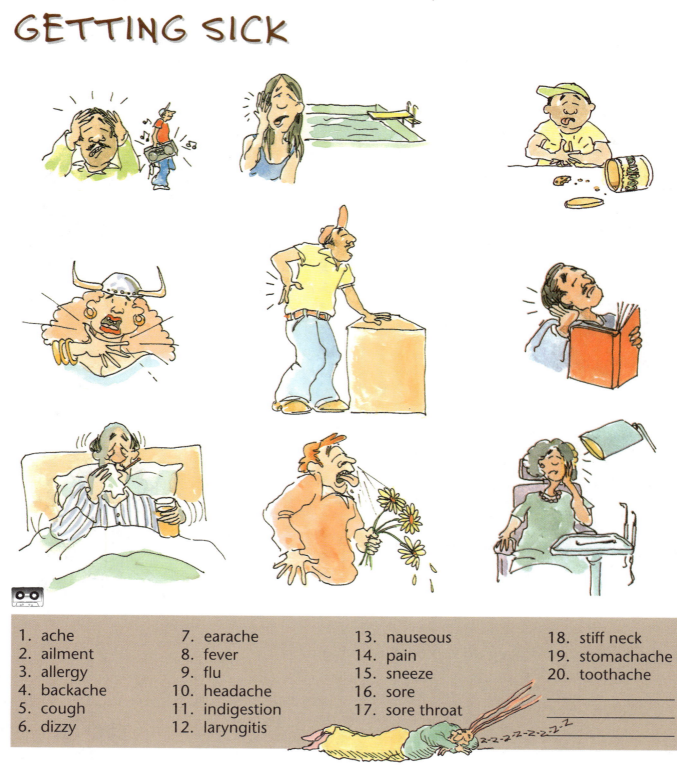

1. ache	7. earache	13. nauseous	18. stiff neck
2. ailment	8. fever	14. pain	19. stomachache
3. allergy	9. flu	15. sneeze	20. toothache
4. backache	10. headache	16. sore	_____
5. cough	11. indigestion	17. sore throat	_____
6. dizzy	12. laryngitis		

Class Discussion
1. What's wrong with these people?
2. How do you treat these common ailments?
3. When do you go to the doctor for these ailments?

Cross-Cultural Exchange
How do people in your country treat these ailments?

See Conversation Springboards on page 212.

Group Game: "What's the matter?"

Work in groups of four or five. • *Pantomime one of these ailments for your group.* • *No speaking!* • *Whoever guesses takes the next turn.*

Partner Activity

Partner's Name _____

Decide what medicines are in this cabinet. • *Fill in the labels.* • *On the empty bottles, write something from YOUR medicine cabinet.* • *Compare your answers with the class.*

155

GOING TO A DOCTOR

➤**ALLERGY**
  Allergy & Immunology Associates
  Arnold, Alan, M.D.
      326 North Ave., Oldtown.........................555-8070
  Wykowski, Carla, M.D.
      4048 E. Wilson Dr., Newtown...............555-7890

➤**CARDIOLOGY**
  Cassidy, James A., M.D.
      57 Park Ave., Oldtown..........................555-1495
      If no answer, call.................................555-8382

➤**DERMATOLOGY**
  Natale, Ellen, M.D.
      2123 S. Main St., Oldtown....................555-3024

➤**EAR, NOSE, & THROAT**
  Wu, Peter M., M.D.
      467 Valley View, Newtown....................555-7974

➤**FAMILY PRACTICE**
  NEWTOWN FAMILY CARE ASSOCIATES
      (New Patients Welcome)
      230 Valley View, Newtown
      Clinics...555-0682
      Garcia, Ana, M.D. 555-9188
      St. Clair, Paul, M.D. 555-3059

➤**GENERAL PRACTICE**
  Henry, Richard, D.O.
      2441 River St., Oldtown........................555-6017
  Johnson, Margaret, M.D.
  General & Family Practice
      94 W. Wilson Dr., Newtown...................555-2198

➤**INTERNAL MEDICINE**
  Hossaini, Ali, M.D.
  Internal Medicine–Family Practice
      212 N. Main St., Oldtown.....................555-9744

➤**NEUROLOGY**
  University Physicians Center
  Brigham, Peter, M.D.
  Papas, Irene, M.D.
      Toll Free.......................................1-800-555-7654
      501 Valley View, Newtown....................555-2341

➤**OBSTETRICS & GYNECOLOGY**
  Birth and Women's Health Center
      376 River St., Oldtown..........................555-7391

➤**ONCOLOGY**
  Oldtown Cancer Center
      127 North Ave., Oldtown.......................555-6090
      Cancer Helpline.........................1-800-555-HELP

➤**OPHTHALMOLOGY**
  Valley Eye & Laser
  Kaplan, Joan, M.D.
  Harris, John, M.D.
      350 E. Wilson Dr., Newtown.................555-2135

➤**PEDIATRICS**
  Rivera, Gloria, M.D.
      417 North Ave., Oldtown.......................555-3338

➤**PSYCHIATRY**
  Bassu, Sadru, M.D.
      (Board Certified)
      438 Park Ave., Suite 6, Oldtown............555-5974

➤**PULMONOLOGY**
  Kehrberg, Martha, M.D.
      617 Valley View, Newtown....................555-3019

➤**RADIOLOGY**
  Jorgensen, Eric, M.D.
      127 North Ave., Oldtown.......................555-6090

Group Decision

Work in groups of five or six. • *Decide which doctor you need.* • *Report your decisions to the class.*

1. You have had a sore throat and a cough for a week. _____
2. You get headaches when you read. _____
3. You think you are pregnant. _____
4. You sneeze a lot when you are outdoors. _____
5. Your baby has a fever and won't eat. _____
6. Your shoulder aches. _____

Partner Role Play 🔘

Make an appointment to see one of the doctors you listed. • One partner is the patient, and the other is the receptionist. • Write a role play. • Present your conversation to the class.

Patient: *Ask these questions (or others):*
1. "When can I see the doctor?"
2. "What do I need to bring?"
3. "Do I have to pay at the visit or can the doctor bill me?"

Receptionist: *Ask these questions (or others):*
1. "Have you ever seen the doctor before?" (If not, "Who recommended the doctor?")
2. "Do you have insurance? Which kind?"

Write

Fill out this form.

PATIENT INFORMATION FORM

Name: _____

Address: _____

_____

Phone number: _____

Insurance: YES _____   NO _____

Name of insurer: _____

Medical problem: (describe) _____

_____

How long have you had this problem? _____

Is it the result of an accident? YES _____   NO _____

(Describe accident): _____

Do you have a fever? YES _____   NO _____

Do you have pain? YES _____   NO _____

Where? _____

Partner Role Play

Partner's Name _____

You are visiting a doctor for the first time. • One partner is the doctor. • The other is the patient. • Write a conversation. • Use the PATIENT INFORMATION FORM. • Present your conversation to the class.

🔘 *See Conversation Springboards on page 212.*

MEDICAL EMERGENCIES

1. accident	7. fall	13. pulse _____
2. cast	8. heart attack	14. stitches _____
3. concussion	9. hurt	15. stomach pump _____
4. electrocardiogram (EKG)	10. ice pack	16. stroke _____
5. emergency room	11. oxygen	17. X-ray _____
6. faint	12. poison	

Class Discussion

Tell the stories together as a class. • What would you do in these situations? • Who has had a medical emergency? • Tell the class what happened.

See Conversation Springboards on pages 212 and 213.

Partner Activity

Decide what to do in these emergencies. • *Report your answers to the class.*

1. If the person sitting next to you on the bus faints, what do you do?
2. If you see someone fall down the stairs, what do you do?
3. If you cut yourself badly with a knife, what do you do?
4. If you step on a rusty nail, what do you do?
5. If you accidentally take poison, what do you do?

Group Decision

Work in groups of five. • *Decide what supplies to use for each of the following emergencies.* • *Report your decisions to the class.*

bee sting	gash	sprained ankle
broken arm	splinter	

Community Activity

Answer these questions with your class. • *Find the missing information and report it to the class.*

1. What is the name of the closest hospital in your neighborhood?
2. Does the hospital have an emergency room? Where is it?
3. Did you ever go to the emergency room? Why?
4. Does your insurance cover emergency room visits?
5. What number do you call for emergencies?

HOSPITAL

1. blood transfusion	7. intensive care unit (ICU)	12. private
2. broken leg	8. intravenous (IV)	13. semi-private
3. coma	9. nurses' station	14. unconscious
4. get-well card	10. orderly	15. visiting hours
5. hospital bed	11. patient	_____
6. information desk		_____

What's the Story?

Work in groups of five. • *Write a story about this hospital scene.* • *Everyone in the group should contribute at least two sentences.* • *Read your story to the class.*

1. Who are the people in this picture?
2. Who is sick? What is wrong?
3. What is the doctor in room 209 doing?
4. What is the patient in room 208 doing? What are the patients in room 209 doing?
5. Who are the visitors? What room are they going to visit?

See Conversation Springboards on page 213.

Class Discussion

What do these signs mean? • Discuss each one.

Partner Activity

Partner's Name _____

Decide which sign in the hospital to follow. • Report your answers to the class.

1. You want to buy a gift for your friend. _____
2. You are hungry and want to get some lunch after your visit. _____
3. You need to get a chest X-ray. _____
4. Your sister is having a baby, and you need a place to wait. _____
5. You have to have a blood test. _____

INSIDE YOUR BODY*

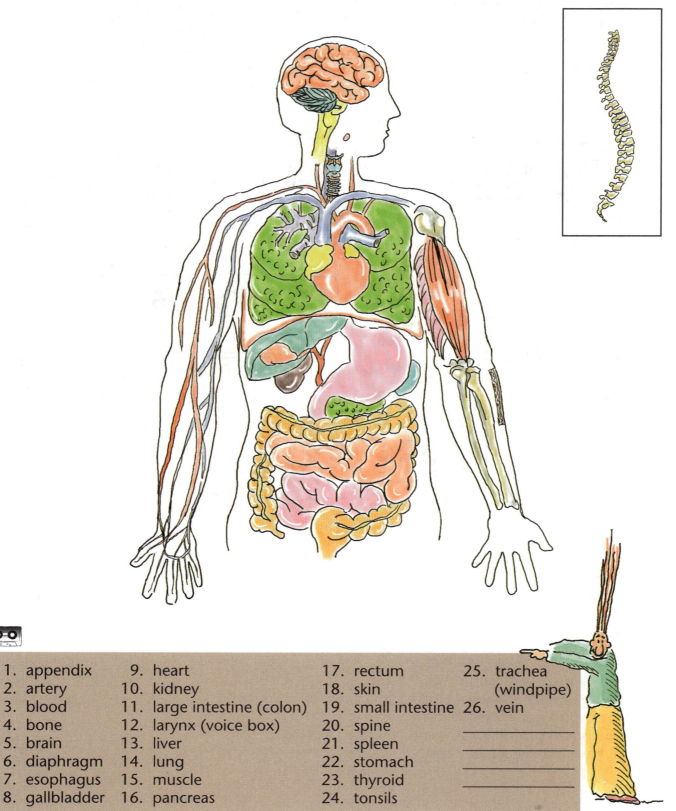

1. appendix	9. heart	17. rectum	25. trachea
2. artery	10. kidney	18. skin	(windpipe)
3. blood	11. large intestine (colon)	19. small intestine	26. vein
4. bone	12. larynx (voice box)	20. spine	_____
5. brain	13. liver	21. spleen	_____
6. diaphragm	14. lung	22. stomach	_____
7. esophagus	15. muscle	23. thyroid	
8. gallbladder	16. pancreas	24. tonsils	

See Conversation Springboards on page 213.

* *See Appendix page 249 for labeled illustration.*

Group Activity

Work in groups of five or six. • *Decide where the problem is.* • *Compare your answers with the class.*

MEDICAL PROBLEM	PART OF THE BODY
1. heart attack	heart
2. tonsillitis	
3. lung cancer	
4. kidney infection	
5. gallstones	
6. appendicitis	
7. broken arm	
8. stroke	
9. tuberculosis	
10. other: _____	

Cross-Cultural Exchange

Compare the treatments for these problems in different countries. • *Which treatments do you prefer?*

Group Game: "Gossip!"

Work in groups of eight. • *Choose a leader.* • *Close your books.* • *Look at the cover.* • *What are the people saying?*

Leader: [*To the first student*] Read the secret on page 247. Close your book. Whisper the secret to the student sitting next to you.

That Student: [*Whisper the secret to the student sitting next to you, etc.*]

Last Student: [*Write the secret on the board or tell the class.*]

Class: [*Check the secret on page 247. Which group had the most accurate secret?*]

THE DENTIST

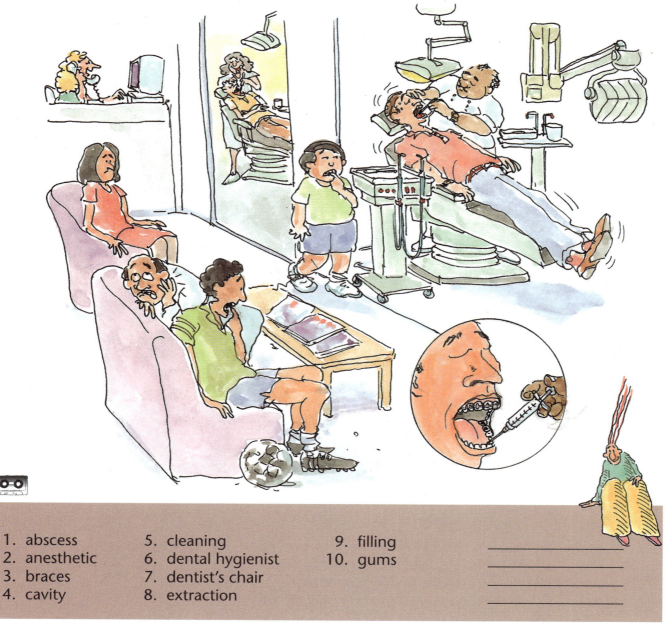

1. abscess
2. anesthetic
3. braces
4. cavity
5. cleaning
6. dental hygienist
7. dentist's chair
8. extraction
9. filling
10. gums

_____
_____
_____
_____

Partner Interview

Partner's Name _____

Practice these questions with your teacher. • *Then ask your partner.*

1. Do you go to the dentist? What is your dentist's name?
2. Where is your dentist's office?
3. Do you like your dentist? Why or why not?
4. Did you ever have a toothache? What did you do?
5. Did you ever wear braces? When?
6. Did you ever get a filling? Did it hurt? Did the dentist give you an anesthetic?

Cross-Cultural Exchange

In your country, when do people go to the dentist? • *What kinds of fillings do people get?*

See Conversation Springboards on pages 213 and 214.

Partner Role Play

You have a toothache and can't eat. • *Call the dentist for an appointment.* • *Present your conversation to the class.*

What's the Story?

Work in groups of five. • *Choose one of the patients on page 164 and write a story about him or her.* • *Everyone in the group should contribute at least two sentences.* • *Read your story to the class.* • *Answer these questions.*

1. What is the patient's name?
2. How old is she/he?
3. Why is this patient at the dentist's office?
4. How does she/he feel? Why?
5. How often does she/he visit the dentist?
6. What will the dentist (or the hygienist) do?
7. Will the dentist give the patient an anesthetic?
8. Does the patient like the dentist? Why or why not?
9. How will the patient feel when she/he leaves the office?
10. Where will she/he go?

Cross-Cultural Exchange

In some cultures, the "Tooth Fairy" takes children's baby teeth from under their pillows and leaves money. • *Is there a special custom in your country for baby teeth?* • *Tell the class.*

THE VETERINARIAN

1. animal	5. dog collar	9. inoculation	13. vet
2. assistant	6. dog tag	10. leash	_____
3. cage	7. examination table	11. license	_____
4. carrying case	8. flea and tick collar	12. rabies tag	_____

Class Discussion

1. Do you have a pet? What kind?
2. What is your pet's name?
3. Did you have a pet when you were a child? What kind?
4. What kind of pet would you like to have? Why?
5. In your country, do people like to have pets? What are the most popular pets in your country?
6. What are some names for pets in your country?
7. Why do people take their pets to the vet?

See Conversation Springboards on page 214.

What's the Story?

Work in groups of five. • *Pick a pet in the picture.* • *Write a story.* • *Everyone in the group should contribute at least one sentence.* • *Read your story to the class.* • *Answer these questions.*

1. What is the pet's name?
2. How old is it?
3. Why is the pet at the vet's office?
4. What will the owner tell the vet?
5. What will the vet tell the owner?
6. What will the owner and the pet do after the visit?

Group Problem Posing/Problem Solving

Work in groups of three or four. • *Choose a situation.* • *State the problem.* • *Find a solution.* • *Report your decision to the class.*

Speech

Tell the class about pets in your country. • *Use these questions as a guide.*

1. Do many people have pets?
2. What are the most popular pets?
3. What are popular names for pets?

REVIEW

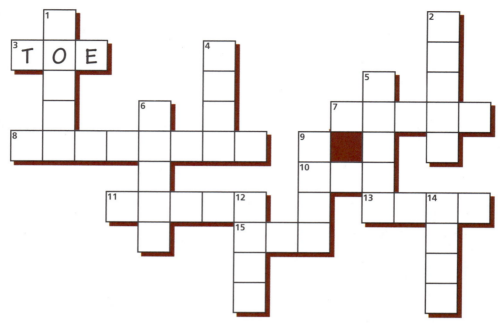

Write

Fill in this crossword puzzle. • *Check your answers with your partner.* ✱

ACROSS

3.

11.

7.

13.

8.

15.

10.

DOWN

1.

6.

2.

9.

4.

12.

5.

14.

✱ *See Appendix page 247 for completed crossword puzzle.*

UNIT 10

LEISURE

LEARNING STRATEGIES

➤ In the Journal section of your notebook, write about your daily leisure activities. For example: I took a walk; I played soccer; I read; I went to a movie.

➤ Find a new leisure activity to practice your English. For example: Watch TV shows in English with a friend. Discuss the shows in English; Take a walk with a friend. Pick a topic and discuss in English.

LEISURE TIME

1. go camping
2. go for a walk
3. go swimming
4. go to a baseball game
5. go to a party
6. go to the movies
7. jog
8. play dominoes
9. play soccer
10. play the guitar
11. play with a pet _____
12. sing a song _____
13. take photographs _____
14. travel _____

Group Vocabulary Challenge

Work in groups of five or six. • *Make a list of leisure-time activities.* • *Read your list to the class.* •
The group with the most activities is the winner!

See Conversation Springboards on page 214.

Group Survey

Ask everyone in your group these questions. • *Check SOMETIMES or NEVER.* • *Count the answers.* • *Report your group's results to the class.* • *Write the class' results on the board.*

In your leisure time, do you . . .	SOMETIMES	NEVER
1. watch TV?	_____	_____
2. go to the movies?	_____	_____
3. read?	_____	_____
4. play with a pet?	_____	_____
5. listen to music?	_____	_____
6. play a musical instrument?	_____	_____
7. watch sports?	_____	_____
8. play a sport?	_____	_____
9. travel?	_____	_____
10. go camping?	_____	_____
11. go to school?	_____	_____

Partner Interview

Partner's Name _____

Practice these questions with your teacher. • *Then ask your partner.*

1. When do you have leisure time?
2. What do you like to do most in your leisure time?
3. What do you like to do on a rainy day?
4. What do you like to do in the summer?
5. What will you do on your next holiday?

What's the Story?

Work in groups of five. • *Write a story for the picture.* • *Everyone in the group should contribute at least one sentence.* • *Read your story to the class.*

GOING OUT

1. amusement park
2. club
3. concert
4. dance
5. dressed up
6. friend
7. guest
8. host
9. museum
10. musician
11. opera
12. painting
13. play
14. religious service
15. roller coaster
16. sculpture _____
17. singer _____
18. theater _____
_____
_____

Class Discussion

What is happening in these pictures? • Discuss each one.

See Conversation Springboards on page 214.

Find Someone Who

What do you like to do when you go out? • *Review the vocabulary with your teacher.* • *Fill in the name of someone who . . .*

1. _____ likes to ride a roller coaster.
2. _____ goes to church every week.
3. _____ likes to visit museums.
4. _____ likes to go to parties.
5. _____ likes to go dancing.
6. _____ likes to go to concerts.
7. _____ goes out with friends every day.
8. _____ has gone to an opera.
9. _____ likes to go to the movies.
10. _____ likes to stay home.

Partner Role Play   Partner's Name _____

Write a telephone conversation. • *One partner invites the other to do something.* • *Present your conversation to the class.*

Community Activity

Bring a local newspaper to class. • *Look in the ENTERTAINMENT section.* • *Are there any interesting events?* • *How much do they cost?* • *Plan a field trip with your class.* • *Enjoy!*

WATCHING TELEVISION

1. antenna
2. cable
3. channel
4. comedian
5. comedy
6. commercial
7. drama
8. game show
9. late-night show
10. program
11. rent a video
12. soap opera
13. talk show
14. variety show

_____
_____
_____
_____

What's the Story?

Work in groups of five. • *Write a story about the picture.* • *Everyone in the group should contribute at least one sentence.* • *Read your story to the class.* • *Who had the funniest story?*

See Conversation Springboards on page 215.

Group Decision

Work in groups of five. • *The people in this picture are looking for a video to watch together.* • *What kind of video does each person prefer?* • *What kind of video will they enjoy together?* • *Report your decision to the class.*

Partner Interview

Partner's Name _____

Practice these questions with your teacher. • *Then ask your partner.*

1. Do you ever rent videos?
2. Where is the best place to rent videos in your neighborhood?
3. What kind of videos do you like?
4. What kind of TV programs do you like?
5. Do you ever watch late-night TV?
6. Which do you like better: to watch TV or to watch videos? Why?

Community Activity

Use a real TV schedule from the newspaper. • *Choose one day of the week.* • *Decide which programs to watch for that day.* • *Write the name, channel, and time of each program.* • *Report your decision to the class.*

MOVIES

1. actor
2. actress
3. aisle
4. audience
5. collect
6. lobby
7. refreshment stand
8. screen
9. sell
10. ticket
11. usher
12. video game

_____
_____
_____
_____

See Conversation Springboards on page 215.

Class Discussion

1. What was the last movie you saw?
2. What movies are in the theaters now?
3. What new movie do you want to see?
4. What do you like to eat and drink at the movies?
5. Do you like to play video games in the lobby of a movie theater?

Group Role Play

Work in groups of four. • *Choose one of these situations.* • *Write a role play.* • *Include roles for everyone.* • *Present your role play to the class.*

1. friends going to a movie together
2. a woman selling tickets
3. a man buying refreshments
4. an usher collecting tickets

Conversation Squares

First write your own answers. • *Then ask your partners about their favorites.* • *Write their answers.* • *Compare your group's answers with other groups.* • *How many students have the same favorites?*

Favorite	You:_____	Partner 1:_____	Partner 2:_____
movie	_____	_____	_____
actor	_____	_____	_____
actress	_____	_____	_____
comedian	_____	_____	_____

INDIVIDUAL SPORTS

1. aerobics
2. bicycling
3. bowling
4. boxing
5. golf

6. gymnastics
7. hiking
8. jogging
9. physical activity
10. running

11. skating
12. skiing
13. swimming
14. tennis
15. wrestling

16. yoga
_____
_____
_____
_____

See Conversation Springboards on page 215.

Group Survey

Ask everyone in your group these questions. • *Write everyone's answers.* • *Compare your group's opinions with the rest of the class.*

Which sport is the . . .

1. most difficult? _____

2. easiest? _____

3. most exciting? _____

4. most dangerous? _____

5. most fun to watch on TV? _____

6. best exercise? _____

Class Game: *"What is your favorite way to exercise?"*

Think. • *Write.* • *Fold your paper.* • *Make a pile of papers.* • *Open one.* • *Ask "What am I doing?"* • *Have the class guess the exercise.*

Community Activity

Where can you enjoy a leisure activity? • *Use the telephone directory.* • *Find out this information.*

Is there a . . .	YES	NO	WHERE?
1. skating rink?	_____	_____	_____
2. bowling alley?	_____	_____	_____
3. swimming pool?	_____	_____	_____
4. tennis court?	_____	_____	_____
5. golf course?	_____	_____	_____
6. ski area?	_____	_____	_____
7. bicycle trail?	_____	_____	_____

TEAM SPORTS

1. base	9. field goal	17. hoop	25. run	30. touchdown
2. baseball	10. football	18. kick	26. score	31. umpire
3. basket	11. foul	19. net	27. shoot	_____
4. basketball	12. free throw	20. out	28. soccer	_____
5. catch	13. goal	21. pass	29. tackle	_____
6. coach	14. goalie	22. pitch		_____
7. down	15. goal post	23. player		_____
8. dribble	16. hit	24. referee		

180

See Conversation Springboards on pages 215 and 216.

Group Discussion

Work in groups of eight. • *Discuss these questions.* • *Report your answers to the class.*

1. Did you ever play on a team? What kind of a team?
2. When did you play?
3. Where did you play?
4. What position did you play?
5. Do you like to watch team sports on TV? What do you like to watch?
6. Do you ever go to sporting events? Which ones do you like to attend?
7. Do you have a favorite team? Which one?

Conversation Squares

First write your own answers. • *Then ask your partners about their favorites.* • *Write their answers.* • *Compare your group's answers with other groups.* • *How many students have the*

Favorite	You:_____	Partner 1:_____	Partner 2:_____
sport	_____	_____	_____
team	_____	_____	_____
player	_____	_____	_____

Community Activity

What sport season is it now? • *Which teams are winning?* • *Choose a game to watch on TV and report to the class.* • *Who played?* • *Who won?* • *What was the final score?* • *What interesting things happened?*

Cross-Cultural Exchange

What is the most popular team sport in your country? • *Who is the most popular sports hero in your country?*

AT THE PARK

1. doll carriage	7. park bench	17. swings
2. feed the birds	8. path	18. water fountain
3. fly a kite	9. picnic basket	13. sandbox
4. have a picnic	10. picnic table	14. see saw
5. jungle gym	11. pigeon	15. slide
6. kite	12. play Frisbee	16. squirrel

Find Someone Who

Review the vocabulary with your teacher. • *Fill in the name of someone who . . .*

1. _____ likes to jog in the park.
2. _____ likes to feed the birds in the park.
3. _____ likes to feed the squirrels in the park.
4. _____ likes to take children to the playground.
5. _____ likes to fly a kite.

See Conversation Springboards on page 216.

Strip Story

Work in groups of four. • *Look at the pictures.* • *Decide what is happening.* • *Tell the story to the class.*

Cross-Cultural Exchange

What do parks look like in your hometown? • *When do people go to the park?* • *What do they do there?* • *What is the name of a famous park in your country?* • *Describe it to the class.*

TAKING A TRIP

1. airplane ticket	6. camera	11. sightseeing	16. travel brochure
2. by airplane	7. luggage/baggage	12. snorkel	_____
3. by boat	8. on a cruise ship	13. suitcase	_____
4. by bus	9. passport	14. (swim) fins	_____
5. by train	10. postcard	15. tour	_____

What's the Story?

Work in groups of three. • Write a story about this picture. • Everyone in the group should contribute at least one sentence. • Read your story to the class.

Group Vocabulary Challenge

Work in groups of three or four. • What would you pack for a trip to a tropical island? • Make a list. • Read your list to the class. • The group with the longest list is the winner!

See Conversation Springboards on page 216.

Group Discussion

Work in groups of five. • *Discuss these questions.* • *Report your answers to the class.*

1. What do you like to do on vacation?
2. How do you prefer to travel?
3. Do you visit your family on vacation? Where do they live?
4. Do you ever travel to another country? Where do you go?
5. Where is the most beautiful place you have ever been?

Write

Imagine you are on vacation. • *Complete the postcard.* • *Address it to your English class.* • *Read it to your class.*

_____
(date)

Hi, _____ !

    Having a wonderful time in _____. I'm

enjoying the _____. The weather is _____.

_____ .

_____

Place stamp here

_____

_____

_____

Cross-Cultural Exchange

What is the best place to visit in your country? • *Tell the class about it.* • *Do you have a postcard or photo of a special place in your country?* • *Bring the postcard or photo to class.* • *Tell the class about the place.* • *Make a bulletin board with everyone's postcards.*

AT THE BEACH

1. beach blanket	8. pail	15. sunbathe	22. waves
2. beach chair	9. sail	16. sunburn	_____
3. beach umbrella	10. sailboat	17. suntan	_____
4. bury	11. sand	18. surf	_____
5. drown	12. sand castle	19. surfboard	_____
6. lifeguard chair	13. shovel	20. swim	_____
7. life preserver	14. speedboat	21. water-ski	_____

What's the Story?

Decide who you would like to be in this picture. • *Write a story.* • *Read your story to the class.*

See Conversation Springboards on pages 216 and 217.

CAMPING

1. backpack	6. lantern	11. sleeping bag	16. wild animal
2. bear	7. porcupine	12. snake	17. wilderness
3. campfire	8. raccoon	13. sunrise	_____
4. deer	9. set up camp	14. tent	_____
5. fox	10. skunk	15. trailer	

Partner Activity

Partner's Name _____

Look at the pictures. • Finish the story. • Write captions. • Compare your story with others in the class.

Class Discussion

1. Do you live near any wild animals? Which ones?
2. What wild animals live in your country?
3. What would you do if any of these animals came near you?

See Conversation Springboards on page 217.

THE LIBRARY

1. author	6. check out	11. librarian	16. subject
2. call card	7. dictionary	12. library card	17. title
3. call number	8. due	13. periodical	_____
4. card catalog	9. encyclopedia	14. return	_____
5. cart	10. late fine	15. stacks (shelves)	_____

Partner Vocabulary Challenge
Partner's Name _____

Make a list of all the people in the library and what they are doing. • *Compare your list with another pair.*

Community Activity

With your class, plan a visit to the library in your school or community. • *Make a list of some questions to ask the librarian.*

See Conversation Springboards on page 217.

SCHOOL

Group Discussion

1. What other courses can you take where you study English?
2. Have you ever taken another course? Which one? When is it offered?
3. Would you like to take another course? What course?
4. Do many adults go to school in your country? What kinds of courses can adults take?

Group Game: "Gossip!"

Work in groups of eight. • *Choose a leader.* • *Close your books.* • *Look at the cover.* • *What are the people saying?*

Leader: [*To the first student*] Read the secret on page 247. Close your book. Whisper the secret to the student sitting next to you.

That Student: [*Whisper the secret to the student sitting next to you, etc.*]

Last Student: [*Write the secret on the board or tell the class.*]

Class: [*Check the secret on page 247. Which group had the most accurate secret?*]

Community Activity

Get a catalog from a school that has courses for adults. • *Pick out courses you would like to take.* • *How much English is required?* • *What did most of the students in the class choose?* • *Sign up and enjoy!*

See Conversation Springboards on page 217.

REVIEW

Partner Interview

Partner's Name _____

Practice these questions with your teacher. • *Then ask your partner.*

1. What is today's date?
2. What is your name?
3. What do you like to do in your leisure time?
4. Where do you prefer to spend your time?
5. How often do you watch TV?
6. What do you watch on TV?
7. What is your favorite physical activity?
8. What would you like to try someday?
9. What do you never want to try?
10. Where would you like to visit someday?

Write

Write about your partner in your journal.

Journal

_____
(1)

My partner's name is _____. When he/she
(2)

has leisure time, he/she likes to _____. He/She
(3)

prefers to spend time _____. He/She watches
(4)

TV _____. When he/she watches TV, he/she prefers
(5)

to watch _____.
(6)

His/Her favorite physical activity is _____. He/She
(7)

would like to try _____ someday, but he/she
(8)

never wants to try _____. He/She would like to
(9)

visit _____ someday.
(10)

Tell the Class

Read your journal to the class. • *Tell the class about your partner.*

Cross-Cultural Exchange

Bring in some typical music from your country. • *Tell the class about the music.* • *Is there a special dance for the music?* • *Teach it to the class.*

190

APPENDIX

CONVERSATION SPRINGBOARDS

UNIT 1: WELCOME TO CLASS

WELCOME TO CLASS! (pp. 2-3)

Conversation 1: *What's happening?*

A: Here's my picture!

B: Oh, I like it. Tell me about it.

A: Well, I'm a woman, of course! I have long, straight hair and green eyes.

B: But your hair is short and curly now.

A: Well, you know, people change. . . Tell me about your picture!

B: All right. Well, of course, I'm a man. I have a moustache and glasses—and brown, wavy hair.

A: But you don't have a moustache now!

B: Well, like you said, people change, you know.

Conversation 2: *What's next?*

A: Hi. I'm Keiko. What's your name?

B: Hi, Keiko. My name's Maria. Nice to meet you.

A: You, too. I like your earrings, Maria.

B: Thanks. They're very old. Keiko, do you know the man with the glasses?

A: Uh-huh.

B: What's his name?

A: That's Paco. He's nice.

B: Would you introduce me?

A: Sure. He's single, you know.

B: Really? Hmm. . .

COUNTRIES (pp. 4-5)

Conversation 1: *What's the process?*

A: Hi. Are you my partner?

B: Yes, I am. What's your name?

A: My name's Paco. What's yours?

B: Don. Don Park. What's your last name, Paco?

A: Montero.

B: How do you spell Montero?

A: M-O-N-T-E-R-O. Where are you from, Don?

B: Seoul, Korea. Where are you from?

A: Colombia. Where's Korea, Don?

B: It's in northern Asia. Where's Colombia?

A: It's in South America. What language do Koreans speak?

B: We speak Korean. What language do Colombians speak, Paco?

A: We speak Spanish.

B: OK. Great! We're finished!

Conversation 2: *What's your opinion?*

A: Where do you want to visit?

B: I want to go to Europe.

A: Where in Europe?

B: Oh, Spain, France, Germany, Italy. . . Actually, I want to see all the countries in Europe.

A: What cities do you want to visit?

B: I want to see Paris. It's so beautiful.

A: You're right, it is. I'm from Paris.

B: Are you really?!

NUMBERS (p. 6)

Conversation: *What's the process?*

A: Let's do a class survey!

B: That sounds like fun! How many students are there?

A: Let's count. Who's absent?

B: No one. We're all here. One, two, three, four, five, six, seven, eight, nine, ten, eleven, twelve—there are twelve of us.

A: Six women and four men, plus us; that's eight women and four men. How many wear glasses?

B: One, two, three, four. Four are wearing glasses.

A: How many men are bald?

B: Zero. Nobody is bald. Everyone has hair.

JOURNAL (p. 7)

Conversation: *What's the process?*

A: Are you ready for our Partner Interview?

B: Yes. You start.

A: OK. What's your name, please?

B: It's Ani Lee. And yours?

A: Sam Young. Nice to meet you, Ani.

B: You, too. What's today's date?

A: April 7th. How many students are in our class?

B: Hmm, I think fifteen. . .

A: Fifty?!

B: No, no! Fifteen.

A: Oh, fifteen. Next question: Are you married?

B: No, I'm single. And you?

A: I'm divorced. OK, next question: Where are you from?

B: I'm from Taipei, Taiwan. What about you?

A: I'm from Pusan, Korea. So, I speak Korean and you speak Chinese, right?

B: That's right. Taiwanese and Mandarin. There, we're done!

CLOTHING AND COLORS (p. 8)

Conversation: *What's the process?*

A: Are you ready for the Partner Game activity, Paul?

B: Sure, Joe. What do we do?

A: You look at my clothes—I look at your clothes—then we sit back to back and list what we remember.

B: OK, that's easy. I'm ready.

A: What do you remember?

B: Let's see. You're wearing a white T-shirt and red shorts.

A: What else?

B: What else? Umm. . . I don't remember the color of your shoes.

A: They're white.

B: Oh, of course—running shoes. OK, now it's your turn.

PAIRS OF CLOTHING (p. 9)

Conversation: *What's next?*

A: Welcome to our fashion show. Here is Maria, our first model.

B: Maria is Brazilian, and today she's wearing a beautiful, light green sweater and gold pants.

192

A: Maria also has on a brown belt and a lovely yellow scarf with polka dots. She has a gold barrette in her hair, and she's wearing green sandals.

Audience: Yea, Maria! Way to go, Maria!

B: Thank you, Maria! Now here's model number two, Adisorn, from Thailand. Adisorn is wearing blue jeans, a purple sweat shirt, and a pair of sneakers with yellow socks.

Audience: All right, Adisorn! Yea!

A: OK. Thanks, Adisorn. Now here's our next model, Olga, from Russia. She's wearing a light pink blouse and red skirt. Her red sunglasses look great with her pretty blouse and skirt.

Audience: Yea! Beautiful! Yea, Olga!

B: All our models have interesting clothes today. Now, who's next?

FAMILY (pp. 10-11)

Conversation 1: *What's happening?*

A: I'm glad you have your family photos today, George. I have mine, too.

B: Great! Tell me about your photos first, Cindy.

A: Well, this one is my whole family: my parents and grandparents, my sister and her family, and me, too.

B: Who's who?

A: Here's my grandmother, and this is my grandfather. And this is my mother, and here's my father.

B: Is this your sister? She's so young!

A: Yes, she's my younger sister. These are her two kids, my niece and nephew.

B: What a great photo! You have a very nice family, Cindy.

Conversation 2: *What's the process?*

A: Let's do the Partner Interview, Chris.

B: All right. You start, Naomi.

A: OK. Is your family big or small?

B: It's small. There are four people in my family.

A: How many brothers and sisters do you have?

B: I have one older brother. No sisters.

A: Do you have any children?

B: No. I'm not married yet. But, I have two dogs and three cats.

A: No kidding! Do you really have five pets?

B: Yes, I do. I love animals!

UNIT 2: EVERYDAY LIFE

THE CLASSROOM (pp. 14-15)

Conversation 1: *What's next?*

A: Hi, Maria. Is it OK if I sit next to you?

B: Sure, Paco, have a seat. I'm reviewing today's lesson from English class. Do you want to review with me?

A: Uh. . . sure. . . good idea.

B: OK. Let's name all the things in the classroom.

A: Let's see. . . There's a big window, a chalkboard, chalk, the teacher's desk, a chair, and a door.

B: Don't forget the clock and the globe, and, of course, desks for all of us!

A: Right! What about things we use?

B: Let's see. . . notebooks, erasers, pens, pencils, paper, and books.

A: Maria, it's fun to study with you.

B: I like it, too, Paco. . .

Conversation 2: *What's the process?*

A: Time for the Group Game, everyone. Yuki, you be the leader.

B: OK. Let me think of something. . . OK, I'm ready.

C: Is it on the board?

B: No, it's not on the board.

D: Is it on the teacher's desk?

B: No, it's not on the teacher's desk.

C: Is it big?

B: Well, not very big. . . It's pretty big.

A: Let's see, it's not on the board, and it's not on the teacher's desk. . . Is it on the wall?

B: Yes, it's on the wall.

A: Is it the clock?

B: Yes, it is! Good guess! You're the new leader now.

TAKING A BREAK (pp. 16-17)

Conversation 1: *What's happening?*

A: Look at Jerry—he's sleeping! He's always tired.

B: Well, he has three jobs. Mark's tired, too. See? He's yawning.

A: Hey, what's wrong with Karen? She's crying!

B: Yeah, she looks pretty upset. Listen to Joe— he's arguing with Vanessa and Tim again. They're always arguing!

A: Unbelievable! But, not Steve. Look—he's laughing. He's always laughing about something.

B: Yeah. Hey, guess who Andrew is drawing on the board!

A: That's funny! Is it George?

B: It sure looks like George. Where is George? I don't see him.

Teacher: OK, class. Break's over.

Conversation 2: *What's next?*

A: I'm glad we're finally taking a break. I'm thirsty!

B: Yeah. It's really hot in the classroom!

A: I need a nice cold glass of water.

B: Me, too!

A: I'm worried tonight. We have a test after the break, you know.

B: I know. I always get nervous about tests.

A: You, too, huh? Oh, my, look at Al! He looks sick!

B: Al, are you OK?

C: Oh. . . I don't know. . .

TIME (pp. 18-19)

Conversation 1: *What's happening?*

A: What time do you go to bed, Gino?
B: Oh, around twelve.
A: Midnight! Are you kidding? That's too late!
B: Well, what time do you go to bed, Sue?
A: About 10:30. I love waking up early and watching the sunrise.
B: Not me! I like studying late at night, going to bed late, and sleeping late.
A: Maybe that's why you're always late to class.
B: And you're always early.
A: Yes, I'm really a morning person.
B: And I'm definitely a night person!

Conversation 2: *What's the process?*

A: OK, guys. Let's do the Group Survey. The class is almost over.
B, C, D: OK. Yeah, sure. All right, let's do it. . .
A: First question: Do you get up early in the morning?
B: Yes, I do.
C: No, I don't.
D: I do.
A: And I do, too. OK, that's three yesses and one no. Question two: Do you get up before 7:00 a.m.?
C: No! Are you kidding?!
B: Yes, I do.
D: I do, too.
A: Me, too. That's three yesses and one no again. Question 3: Do you go to bed late at night? (*Bell rings.*)
B: Time to go!
A: Come on, guys. Let's finish this question.
C: Yeah, what's the hurry?
D: We have a class—we want to be on time!

EVERYDAY LIFE (pp. 20-21)

Conversation 1: *What's the process?*

A: Our daily lives are so different, Lucy. You have five kids, and you're here on time for class every day!
B: Yep, that's my life, Charlie.
A: How do you do it? I'm single and I'm always late!
B: Well, I get up early. The children go to school early. Then I do the housework. At 8:00 I go to school. No problem.
A: No problem for you!
B: What about you, Charlie?
A: Me? I sleep late because I study late at night. When do you do your homework, Lucy?
B: I do mine late at night, too. I guess our lives are the same in one way.

Conversation 2: *What's the process?*

Teacher: OK, class, this activity is called Find Someone Who. Let's try one together. Tom, do you wash the dishes every evening?
A: No way! My wife does the dishes!
Teacher: How about you, Rita? Do you wash the dishes every evening?
B: No, I don't. I make dinner, and my kids wash the dishes.

Teacher: Jerry, do you wash the dishes every evening?
C: Yes, I do. My wife works at night, and I make dinner and wash the dishes.
Teacher: Good. Now fill in Jerry's name on the line. J-E-R-R-Y. Any questions?
Students: No. I'm fine. No problem.
Teacher: OK. Stand up, walk around, and ask questions. Sit down when you're finished. You have ten minutes.

MORNING ROUTINE (pp. 22-23)

Conversation 1: *What's happening?*

A: The guy in the book is so funny! Do you have the same morning routine as he does, Anna?
B: No, my morning routine is very different.
A: How?
B: Well, first of all, I always get up really early, at five o'clock.
A: That *is* early!
B: And, of course, I don't shave. I usually take a bath, not a shower.
A: Do you always make your bed?
B: Sometimes. Do you?
A: No, I never make my bed!

Conversation 2: *What's happening?*

A: Do you watch the morning news on TV, Sally?
B: Sometimes. I like to watch the news and drink my coffee. What about you, Mohammed?
A: I never watch the morning news. I'm always in a hurry.
B: Why?
A: Because I don't like to get out of bed in the morning.
B: I like to stay in bed sometimes, too. I like to watch TV in bed.
A: You, too? I always watch TV in bed. But I never watch the news.
B: No? Well, I watch the news and drink my coffee in bed. *Then* I get up.

UNIT 3: THE CALENDAR

DAYS OF THE WEEK (pp. 26-27)

Conversation 1: *What's the process?*

A: You're my partner, Henry. Where's your calendar?
B: Here it is, but I don't understand what to do. Can you help me?
A: Yeah, sure. Start with yesterday, Sunday. What did you do?
B: I visited my family in the afternoon, and I studied in the evening.
A: OK. Write "visit family" in the Sunday afternoon box. All right. Now write "study" in the Sunday evening box.
B: I see. Thanks. So, today, Monday, I write "class" in the Monday morning box, "lunch with friends" in the afternoon box, and "work" in the evening box. Right?
A: Exactly! Not so hard, is it?
B: No, I guess not. Thanks, Jim!

194

Conversation 2: *What happened?*

A: What did you do last weekend, Al?

B: Oh, nothing special. I worked Saturday. Then, yesterday, I studied most of the day, and watched the basketball game on TV last night. What about you, Becky?

A: Your weekend sounds wonderful to me, Al! Mine was terrible.

B: Really? What happened?

A: Well, Friday evening I had a big fight with my boyfriend. Saturday I had a headache all day, and I felt terrible.

B: Gee, I'm sorry. What about Sunday?

A: Well, I wanted to study Sunday, but I lost my English book. So, I didn't do my homework, and now I don't have a book!

B: Really? I found an extra English book in my backpack this weekend. See? There's no name in it. Maybe it's yours.

A: Oh, it *is* my book! That's my writing in the vocabulary boxes! Thank you, Al. You made my day!

MONTHS AND DATES (pp. 28-29)

Conversation 1: *What's the process?*

A: OK, group, what are some important dates?

B: Hmm. . . Let's see. How about this one: January 1st—the first day of the year.

A: That's a good one. What are some others?

C: How about February 14th? It's Valentine's Day.

A: Great! Now we have two dates. Let's get some more.

D: I know one. November 17th is a very important day!

B: November 17th? That's today. Why is today so important?

D: It's my first anniversary!

A, B, C: Happy anniversary!

Conversation 2: *What's your opinion?*

A: What's your favorite month, Bill?

B: I don't know. I don't think I have a favorite month, Pete. Do you?

A: Yeah, June is my favorite month. My birthday's June third.

B: Really?! My birthday's on the third, too, but July third.

A: There's another reason I like June best. I always take my vacation then—the second week in June. By the way, do you know what date this course ends?

B: Yes, June ninth.

A: Great! I'll start my vacation on June tenth.

B: I usually take my vacation in July. You know, I guess I do have a favorite month—July!

BIRTHDAYS (pp. 30-31)

Conversation 1: *What's happening?*

A: Let's hurry and finish up. She's coming home soon.

B: Quick, Jan! Light the candles!

C: No, not yet. It's too soon.

D: Oh! There are no cups on the table! And where are the napkins?

C: Don't worry, they're right here.

D: OK.

A: Oh, no! She's here! She's at the door!

B: But the candles, the candles! (*Door opens.*)

A, B, C, D: Surprise!
(*singing*)
Happy birthday to you,
Happy birthday to you,
Happy birthday, dear Teacher,
Happy birthday to you.

Conversation 2: *What's the process?*

A: When's your birthday, Raymond?

B: August 20th. When's yours?

A: February 28th. What's a good message for a birthday card?

B: I don't know. "Happy birthday," I guess.

A: But it already says "happy birthday." I want to write something more, something special.

B: How about. . . umm. . . I got it! How about this: "You're a very special friend. Have a great birthday!"

A: I like it! How do you spell "special"?

B: S-p-e. . . uh. . . How about "You're a very good friend," instead?

A: Fine. I know how to spell that.

HOLIDAYS (pp. 32-33)

Conversation 1: *What's the process?*

A: OK, I'm finished writing. These Conversation Squares are easy.

B: I'm ready, too. Let's ask the questions now.

C: Not yet! I'm not finished!

A: That's OK, Sue. Take your time. Christina and I can begin. What's your favorite holiday, Christina?

B: Halloween. I love Halloween parties! Every year I wear a different costume. Last year I was an ugly witch.

A: Good. That's a "holiday activity." What about "holiday food"?

B: Hmm. . . The only special food I know for Halloween is candy. Is that OK?

A: Sure.

C: OK, I'm ready now. What did you say, Christina?

Conversation 2: *What's the process?*

A: Can you help me with the speech I'm giving today?

B: Sure, I'd be glad to. Let's see, the topic is "Holidays in My Country." What holiday do you want to talk about?

A: Hmm. . . How about Independence Day?

B: Sounds good. What happens on that day?

A: Well, there's no work or school. Everyone has a day off.

B: Right, but what are the customs?

A: There's always a parade with marching bands, and families get together.

B: What about fireworks?

A: I almost forgot! That's my favorite thing—I always watch the fireworks!

SEASONS (pp. 34-35)

Conversation 1: *What's happening?*

A: What are the seasons like in your hometown, Maria?

B: Oh, they are very different from here. Remember, I come from Brazil!

A: So, what are the seasons like in Brazil?

B: Well, summer is in December, January, and February. So, Christmas is very hot and sunny.

A: That *is* very different! Summer in my country is June, July, and August. What's winter like in Brazil?

B: It depends on where in Brazil. Some places are cold and rainy, and some are just cool.

A: Does it snow?

B: Not really. If we want snow, we go to Chile.

Conversation 2: *What's the process?*

A: OK, it's time to close the book now. What do you remember from the picture, Elizabeth?

B: Not much, Linda.

A: Why? We looked at the picture.

B: Oh, I remember the picture. But I forget the words. Vocabulary is very difficult for me.

A: Ah, I understand. I'll start, then. You write the words. You know, writing is good practice for vocabulary.

B: OK, good idea. So, what do you remember, Linda?

A: I remember a frozen man in a big block of ice.

B: And I remember a snowman!

A: You do remember vocabulary! That's great, Liz!

WEATHER (pp. 36-37)

Conversation 1: *What's the process?*

A: OK, Partner Interview again. Of course, I know your name already, Kati. Let me write it in. . .

B: I'll start, OK? What do you like to do on a rainy day, Jun?

A: I like to stay in bed and read all day. I feel lazy on a rainy day! What do you like to do on a rainy day, Kati?

B: Believe it or not, I like to go out for a walk in the rain. I take my dog with me. She likes it, too!

A: Really?! Don't you get wet?

B: A little. But I wear my raincoat, and I have an umbrella. My dog wears a raincoat, too! It's fun, really. Why don't you come with us next time?

A: No, thanks. I think I'll stay in bed. (*Bell rings.*)

B: Oh, no—the bell! We never get to finish!

Conversation 2: *What happened?*

A: How was your weekend, Gene?

B: Crazy! I had a real adventure! My family and I were on a picnic, and there was a hailstorm!

A: Oh, no! What did you do?

B: We hid under the picnic table. The hail was as big as golf balls!

A: You're kidding!

B: No, really. We ate lunch under the table.

A: I had an adventure in the desert one time. I was riding a horse, and there was a dust storm.

B: Oh, no! What did you do?

A: Well, my horse stopped, of course. I just closed my eyes and hid my face and waited for the storm to pass. It was awful! I couldn't breathe!

B: It sounds worse than a hailstorm!

WEATHER REPORT (p. 38)

Conversation: *What's next?*

Meteorologist: . . . And the weather for the Northwest today was cloudy and cool.

A: Boy, I'm glad we don't live in the Northwest. It's always cloudy and cool there!

B: And rainy!

A: This is my kind of weather here—hot and sunny all summer!

Meteorologist: Tomorrow, the Northeast is getting severe thunderstorms.

A: Oh, no! I want to go to the beach tomorrow!

B: Me, too. Maybe the meteorologist is wrong.

A: Well, if he's right, let's go to the movies!

SEASONAL CLOTHING (p. 39)

Conversation: *What's happening?*

A: This is my first winter here in Boston. It's so cold, and I don't know what to wear!

B: I see that, Joshua! You're shivering! You definitely need a heavy winter jacket.

A: I think you're right, Jenny. This jacket was fine in my country, but this weather is too cold and windy for it!

B: Buy some gloves and boots and a wool hat, too. Some people like earmuffs instead of hats.

A: What about long underwear?

B: If it's very cold and you're outdoors, long underwear is a good idea.

A: Thanks for the advice, Jenny. But when does it get warm here?

B: *Really* warm? Not for five more months! Put away your shorts and bathing suits until June!

UNIT 4: FOOD

FRUIT (pp. 42-43)

Conversation 1: *What's next?*

A: What's your favorite fruit, Jeff?

B: Oh, I love all kinds of fruit, Gail.

A: Me, too. But what do you like best?

B: Well, I think maybe oranges.

A: Mmm. I like oranges, too. What other fruits do you like?

B: Grapefruit. I love grapefruit. And cherries—but I don't like the pits.

A: How about grapes and watermelon?

B: Yes, but not the seeds. I like seedless grapes and seedless watermelon better. Boy, this conversation is making me hungry for some fruit!

A: Me, too!

Conversation 2: *What's the process?*

A: Hey, let's make a fruit salad!

B, C, D: Great idea! Sounds good! Yeah!

B: OK. We can each bring something for the salad.

C: I'll bring a bowl and a large spoon.
D: I'll bring a knife—I have a sharp knife.
B: I'll bring plates and forks.
A: What about the fruit? My favorites are oranges and grapefruit.
D: Mmm-hmm! And I love melons—watermelon and cantaloupe!
C: Don't forget grapes and bananas and apples.
B: Bring everything tomorrow, and we'll make the fruit salad for lunch.
A, C, D: Yum! Sounds great! All right!

VEGETABLES (pp. 44-45)

Conversation 1: *What's happening?*

A: Hi. Can I help you?
B: Yes. What vegetables are good today?
A: Let's see. . . everything is good, but the corn and the cabbage are especially fresh.
B: That corn does look good! I'll take a half dozen ears, please.
A: Yes, the corn is a good buy. It's in season. Anything else?
B: The tomatoes look great. I'll take four. And a head of lettuce.
A: How about some beans? They just came in this morning.
B: OK. A pound of beans. That's all for today. By the way, what's your dog's name?
A: Veggie. He loves all kinds of vegetables. Here, Veggie, want a carrot?
Dog: Woof! Woof!

Conversation 2: *What's the process?*

A: We'd like to show you our salad. This is how we made it. We each brought in a different vegetable and prepared it together.
B: I brought in a head of lettuce.
C: Carol and I washed the lettuce. Then I shredded it and put it in the bowl.
D: I brought in a bunch of carrots. I peeled them and cut them up.
C: I cooked the beets and sliced them at home.
A: I don't like vegetables, but I brought in some mushrooms, anyway.
D: We mixed all the vegetables together, and then we added salad dressing.
B: And here it is! We hope you enjoy it!

MEAT, SEAFOOD, AND POULTRY (pp. 46-47)

Conversation 1: *What's next?*

A: I'm glad you're coming for dinner tonight, Paco. Do you eat poultry?
B: Do you mean chicken?
A: Yes, chicken or turkey. Which do you prefer? Or would you prefer red meat?
B: Well, Maria, I don't really eat red meat.
A: I don't eat much red meat, either. How about some seafood? Fish? Shrimp?
B: Well. . . I don't really care too much for fish, either, Maria.

A: That's OK. How about pork chops, then?
B: Actually, Maria, I'm a vegetarian. I don't usually eat any meat at all. But I know I'll like anything you cook!

Conversation 2: *What's the process?*

A: Karen, do you understand this Find Someone Who?
B: I think so.
A: We need to find classmates who like food a certain way, right?
B: Yes. Let's start with you, Don. Do you like baked fish with salt and pepper?
A: Well, I like salt and pepper, but I don't like baked fish!
B: OK. Now I'll ask Steve. Oh, Steve, do you like baked fish with salt and pepper?
C: Yes, I love it! Now, let me ask you and Don Question Two. Do you like barbecued spare ribs?
B: What's that?
C: I'm not sure! Do you know what they are, Don?
A: Yeah, I think they're. . . umm. . . Let's ask the teacher.

DESSERTS (pp. 48-49)

Conversation 1: *What's the process?*

A: How do we do this activity?
B: First, we fill in the menu with desserts we all like.
C: I'll start with brownies. And what about the prices?
D: Let's fill in all the desserts first, and then do the prices.
B: OK. How about apple pie with ice cream?
A: That's called apple pie a la mode. Let's add sherbet.
C: And frozen yogurt. That's popular these days.
D: How many desserts do we have now?
A: Four. We need one more. How about some chocolate chip cookies?
B: Great! The menu's ready. Oh, wait a minute! We didn't do the prices! (*Bell rings*.)
Teacher: That's it for today. We'll continue this activity tomorrow—same groups.

Conversation 2: *What's your opinion?*

A: This looks like a great class! Look at all those desserts!
B: Here's the dessert I brought in. It's called "anpan." It's a pastry filled with red bean paste. It's from Japan.
C: That looks delicious. Mine is from Puerto Rico. It's "flan."
D: Well, look at mine! It looks the same. It's called "crème brûlée" and is very popular in France.
C: It does look the same as mine! What's in it?
D: It's made with milk and eggs. It's a custard.
C: It *is* the same! I can't wait to taste it!
Teacher: I know you are all waiting for this: break time!
Students: Oh, great! Delicious! Mmm! Wonderful!

BREAKFAST (pp. 50-51)

Conversation 1: *What's your opinion?*

A: What do you eat for breakfast, Paul?

B: Not much, really. Usually I have a glass of orange juice and vitamins. I always take vitamins in the morning.

A: Do you eat anything else for breakfast?

B: Sometimes I have a piece of toast.

C: I always have a big breakfast: eggs, bacon, home fries, coffee, and juice. I love American breakfasts.

A: I do, too, Sam, but they make me fat.

C: What do you eat for breakfast, Kathy?

A: I have juice, nonfat yogurt, and toast. It's better for my health.

Conversation 2: *What's the process?*

A: Conversation Squares again! OK, first we write our own answers.

B: I wrote my answers already.

C: Me, too.

A: All right. Let's ask the questions, then. What did you have for breakfast today, Van Yen?

B: I had noodle soup.

A: Noodle soup! Really?

B: Oh, yes. It's very good. I always have noodle soup for breakfast. What did you have, Jack?

A: Hot cereal and cocoa. It's my favorite in the winter. I have it every day. What about you, Mimi?

C: Just a cup of coffee. I never eat anything for breakfast.

A: So we each have the same breakfast every day.

C: Yes, but we don't all have the *same* breakfast!

LUNCH (pp. 52-53)

Conversation 1: *What's happening?*

A: I'm so hungry! I skipped lunch today, and now I'm really hungry!

B: I never skip lunch, Ken.

A: Well, I'm sorry I did. What did you have for lunch, Jim?

B: Spaghetti and meatballs.

A: That sounds wonderful! Where did you go for lunch?

B: Oh, I just ate at work. We have a microwave oven there. I always bring in leftovers and warm them up.

A: That's a good idea. Do you like to cook?

B: No, but my mother is a great cook. She always makes lots of food, and I have leftovers for lunch.

A: Lucky you! Does your mother want another son?

Conversation 2: *What's happening?*

A: What's for lunch, Paco?

B: Sandwiches.

A: Oh, good. I love sandwiches.

B: What would you like on yours, Maria?

A: What do you have?

B: Everything—cold cuts, tuna fish, cheese, peanut butter—you name it! We have three kinds of bread, too.

A: Great! Do you have sliced turkey?

B: Sure do. What kind of bread? White? Wheat? Rye?

A: Rye, please. And could I have some lettuce, tomato, and mayonnaise with that?

B: You bet.

A: What a beautiful sandwich! Thanks, Paco.

FAST FOOD (pp. 54-55)

Conversation 1: *What's the process?*

A: Do you think fast food is bad for you, Heather?

B: Yes, of course. I like fast food, but I know it's bad for me.

A: OK, that's it! We're finished with the Group Survey questions.

C: Now we count the answers, right?

A: Right. I have four "yesses" and three "nos" for Number 1.

B: No, that's not right! I have three "yesses" and four "nos."

C: And I have four "yesses" and four "nos"!

D: That can't be right. There are only seven people in our group. What do we do now?

C: Count again. Or ask the questions again, raise our hands, and count together.

A, B, D: Oh, boy! Not again!

Conversation 2: *What's the process?*

A: Role plays are difficult to write, aren't they?

B: Do you think so? I think they're easy.

A: Easy? Really? I'm glad you're my partner, Victor.

B: OK. Let's see now. . . The cashier says "May I help you?"

A: Why doesn't he say "Can I help you?"

B: Because it says "May I help you" in the book.

A: But is "Can I help you?" OK? I hear people say "Can I help you?" in stores all the time.

B: Yes, that's true. You can say that. But I think "May I help you?" is a little more polite.

A: Really? But, can we change it, anyway?

B: I think I understand why role plays are difficult for you to write, Lisa.

JUNK FOOD (p. 56)

Conversation: *What's next?*

A: Coffee break! Junk food time! I'm going to the vending machines. Want something, Bob?

B: No thanks, Mary.

A: Don't you ever eat junk food?

B: Not from these vending machines!

A: Why not?

B: Last week I lost money in the machine three times! Nothing came out—no soda, no coffee, no money back.

A: That's too bad! What did you do?

B: I kicked the machine a few times, but nothing happened.

A: Well, I hope it works today. I'm really hungry for a chocolate bar! Wish me luck!

DINNER (p. 57)

Conversation: *What's next?*

A: I'm glad we came to this restaurant, David. It's beautiful!

B: It *is* nice, isn't it? Margaret, there's something I want to talk to you about.

A: Really? What is it, David?

B: Well, we've known each other for three years now.

A: Uh-huh.

B: And we like each other. . . a lot.

A: Yes, we do.

B: Well, I. . .

C: David! Margaret! What a surprise! Hey, Annie, it's David and Margaret! Oh, this is great! Let's have dinner together!

D: Wait, Jack—maybe David and Margaret want to eat alone.

B: No, no. . . that's. . . that's fine, Annie. It's. . . it's good to see you, *really*.

THE SUPERMARKET (pp. 58-59)

Conversation 1: *What's happening?*

A: You push the cart, OK? Thanks, honey.

B: Sure. What's on the shopping list?

A: Let's see. . . bread, pickles, eggs, ketchup.

B: How much bread do we need?

A: Oh, one loaf is fine, dear. And just a small jar of pickles.

B: OK. Which aisle are the pickles in?

A: Aisle Two. And get a dozen eggs, honey. They're at the end of the aisle.

B: A large bottle of ketchup, right?

A: Yes, I love ketchup! Thanks for shopping with me today, dear. It's fun to shop together, isn't it? . . . Dear? I said, isn't it fun to shop together?

B: Oh, yes, right. Lots of fun. . .

Conversation 2: *What's the process?*

A: What's this Vocabulary Challenge activity?

B: We have to make a list of things from the supermarket.

C: And work fast.

A: That sounds easy. But I don't want to write the words. I can't spell.

C: OK, I'll write. What are some things?

Students: Milk, meat, fish, oranges, apples, margarine, napkins, salt, pepper, rice, potatoes. . . Don't forget lettuce, carrots, beans, celery, chicken, turkey, mayonnaise, cookies. . .

C: Wait a minute, wait a minute! I can't write that fast! Now start again. What did you say—milk? (*Buzzer sounds.*)

Teacher: OK, class. Time's up. How many words do you have?

UNIT 5: HOMES

CITY OR COUNTRY (pp. 62-63)

Conversation 1: *What's next?*

A: First question on the Group Discussion. Do you like where you live now?

B: Yes, I do.

C: I don't. I liked my hometown better.

D: I do. I love living here.

A: And my answer is yes, too. OK. Second question: In your opinion, where is the best place in the world to live?

D: Definitely Alaska. You can ski all the time!

B: I think right here. I love the city—it's so exciting.

C: No, I hate the city. It's so noisy! The best place is in the country. It's calm and peaceful.

A: Or by the ocean. I love the water. I'd like to live on the coast.

B: Uh-oh. The last question asks us to decide as a group which place we like best. How will we ever agree on that?!

Conversation 2: *What's the process?*

A: Time for the "Gossip!" game. This will be fun! OK, we need to choose a leader. How about if Pat is the leader?

Students: Sure! OK. Great!

B: Now, everyone, close your books. Tom, you read the secret on page 247. . .

C: OK. I read it. Now what?

B: Now tell the secret to the person sitting next to you; tell Maria the secret.

C: I came to the U.S. when I was 15 with my mother and father and two brothers. We lived on a busy street in the city. Our street was noisy. It was exciting to be in a big city because I was born on a farm in the country. I still love the city.

B: Now, Maria, tell the person next to you. Remember to whisper!

D: I was born in the countryside. It was beautiful and quiet. I moved to the U.S. when I was 15. We lived in the city. It was noisy. I still love the city.

B: OK, great. Now, Kan, tell the next person.

E: I love the city even though it's noisy and dirty. I was born in a beautiful town in the country. Umm. Boy, this is hard. I can't remember all the details!

HOMES (pp. 64-65)

Conversation 1: *What's your opinion?*

A: What do you think of the homes around here?

B: Well, they sure are different from the homes in the place where I was born.

A: Why? What do you mean?

B: Well, in my hometown, all the homes were private homes. And most of them were made of stucco.

A: Did you have a yard and a porch?

B: Yes. Actually, my parents still live there. There's a balcony, too.

A: Wow. It sounds beautiful. Here there are so many apartments and condos! And we live in dormitories! Hardly a private house at all.

B: Yes, and out on the highway, there are so many mobile home parks.

A: Well, that's a lot different from the neighborhood where I grew up.

Conversation 2: *What's happening?*

A: What do you think of the new high-rise in our neighborhood?

B: I really like it! I saw a model apartment. The floors are all wood, and there are fireplaces in every apartment!

A: And some of the apartments have balconies. I think there's a terrace garden on the roof, too.

B: There are trees and flowers—on the roof!

A: Do you think there's a basement? A lot of new buildings don't have basements!

B: Are you kidding? In this building they have everything! It's like having your own house!

A: I guess so, but I'd rather have my own little house to call home.

B: Not me. I wish I had enough money—I'd live in that new place!

THE KITCHEN (pp. 66-67)

Conversation 1: *What's next?*

A: Your kitchen is so different from mine, Maria!

B: Well, there are some things that are the same.

A: Yes, we both have a refrigerator, a stove, and a sink. But you have a microwave. . . and a dishwasher.

B: I know. I love modern conveniences. I just bought an electric rice cooker!

A: Where will you put it? You don't have much counter space.

B: I'll find the space. I make rice every day.

A: You're a good cook, Maria. I remember that wonderful vegetarian dinner you cooked for me.

B: Well, you make a great sandwich!

A: That's about all I can make in my tiny kitchen. I eat out a lot. Hey, do you want to grab a bite to eat now?

Conversation 2: *What happened?*

A: What's your favorite room in your house, Erin?

B: Definitely the kitchen.

A: Really? Why?

B: When I was a child, the kitchen was the center of my family's life.

A: I remember that my mother was always busy in the kitchen.

B: Mine, too. And we all did our homework at the kitchen table.

A: So did we. It was great to be near the snacks!

B: My mother always kept an eye on us so we wouldn't fool around!

THE DINING ROOM (pp. 68-69)

Conversation 1: *What happened?*

A: Do you have a dining room in your house?

B: Are you kidding? I have a small apartment!

A: I meant, did you have a dining room when you were a child?

B: No, we didn't. Did you?

A: Yes. We ate dinner there every night.

B: What was it like?

A: It was pretty formal. It had a glass table and eight chairs. My mom taught us how to set the table. First,

we always put a white tablecloth on the table. Then we put the plates, silverware, glasses, and napkins on the table.

B: Sounds pretty formal. We ate in the kitchen at a large, round table.

A: I bet you had more fun!

Conversation 2: *What's the process?*

A: Do you want to do the Group Role Play together?

B: Sure. Let's get three more. Carlos, do you want to be in our group?

C: Sure. How about Ted and Chet?

D: Sure.

E: All right.

A: OK, which scene should we choose?

C: Let's do the teenager one.

A, B, D, E: Sure. That's fine. Let's get started. What do we do first?

B: Well, what should the names be? How about Al? Jennifer?

C: Tiffany? Chuck?

D: And Pete? That's five.

E: OK. Now how do they feel? That's a weird question. What does it mean?

B: I think that means, do they feel hungry or tired or happy or sad.

A: Right! Let's decide what they are going to say. . .

THE LIVING ROOM (pp. 70-71)

Conversation 1: *What's the process?*

Teacher: Time for the Class Game: "What do you do in the living room?" Write what you do on a piece of paper.

A: Let me see. What do I do? Hmm. . .

B: Oh, I know. . .

Teacher: OK, everyone. Fold your papers. Now come up together. Make a pile of papers. Who wants to be first?

C: I do.

Teacher: OK, Jason. Pick one. Do a pantomime. Ask the class, "What am I doing?"

C: OK. What am I doing?

A: Listening to a CD.

C: Nope.

D: I know. He's studying and watching TV at the same time!

C: You guessed it! Your turn!

Conversation 2: *What's the process?*

A: Do we all have our ads from furniture stores for the Community Activity?

Students: Yes. I have mine! Yep.

A: Let's make a list of things for a living room. We'll start with a couch, OK?

B: And, of course, a stereo with a CD player!

C: Let's include a CD collection, too!

D: How about a TV? I know—an entertainment center! That includes the TV, VCR, and stereo.

E: How about two comfortable armchairs and a coffee table, too?

200

C: Let's add a nice rug and drapes.

B: Don't forget the lamps. And pictures for the walls!

A: We'd better stop here. Let's try to add up the bill. This is a pretty fancy living room!

THE BEDROOM (pp. 72-73)

Conversation 1: *What's the process?*

A: What was your childhood bedroom like?

B: Well, it wasn't very big. I shared it with my sister.

A: How many windows did it have?

B: It had one window. We had pink curtains on the window.

A: What furniture was in the room?

B: Let's see. We had our own beds, and each bed had a night stand. We each had our own desk, but we shared a dresser.

A: Was there a closet?

B: The closet! We had everything in that closet: games, dolls, toys, clothes, shoes. We also kept our secret letters and diaries there! And we never cleaned it! It was a mess!

Conversation 2: *What's happening?*

A: How many bedrooms are in your house?

B: We have three bedrooms: one for my parents, one for my two brothers, and one for me.

A: Tell me about your room.

B: It's a pretty big room. There's a blue bedspread on the bed and curtains to match.

A: Do you spend a lot of time in your room?

B: Oh, yes. I have a stereo and a TV. There's a carpet on the floor. It's very cozy.

A: You're lucky to have your own room. I share my bedroom with my younger sister. We have a telephone in our room, and we're always fighting over it.

B: Well, you're lucky to have a sister to fight with!

THE BATHROOM (p. 74)

Conversation: *What's happening?*

A: In the morning, the bathroom is the busiest room in our house!

B: That's because we're all rushing to get out in the morning. One bathroom is not enough!

C: OK, I've showered. I'll take my electric razor into the bedroom to shave. Next.

A: My turn!

D: No, mine!

B: Jenni, let your brother go first. He's faster! Take your toothbrush and toothpaste into the kitchen.

D: OK. I'm in a rush today. Just hurry up, Kevin!

A: I'll try, but I have to take a shower and wash my hair.

E: I have to use the toilet! I have to use the toilet!

B: I'll go last. I'm not working today. I'm going to take a nice bubble bath when you all leave!

AT HOME (p. 75)

Conversation: *What's the process?*

A: Time for a Group Survey, guys. Is everyone ready?

B: Let's try to get this one done. We never finish.

C: Is it OK if I ask the questions?

A, B, D: Sure. Fine. Let's get going.

C: How often do you eat lunch at home?

D: I never eat lunch at home.

B: I eat lunch at home every day. I live near the school.

A: Sometimes I eat at home, but sometimes I eat at school. I eat out a lot, too. I love sandwiches for lunch. That reminds me, I'm hungry.

C: Peter, you can eat later. We have to finish this survey!

Teacher: Time's up! Let's start to report back.

NEIGHBORS (pp. 76-77)

Conversation 1: *What's the process?*

A: Let's try this Partner Interview, Rex. I'll fill in your name and you fill in mine.

B: OK, Emi. You start asking the questions.

A: How many neighbors do you know?

B: I don't know any of my neighbors. They're very unfriendly. One has a big, ugly dog. I'm afraid of the dog and I'm afraid of the neighbor.

A: That's a shame. Is the dog on a leash?

B: No, it's not. That's why I'm afraid. I always think it'll bite me.

A: You know, my uncle lives near you—and he has a big German Shepherd named Killer.

B: Oh, no! That's the dog! That's my neighbor!

Conversation 2: *What's next?*

A: Are you still having problems with your next-door neighbors?

B: Yes, I'm afraid so. I just found out yesterday that their son, John, borrowed my son's bicycle without telling him.

A: That's terrible.

B: And now, Marge, John's mother, is gossiping to the other neighbors about us. She said that they lent my husband their snow shovel last winter, and he never returned it.

A: You're kidding. You always lend things to them!

B: I know. We always help them. I even baby-sat for John when he was a little baby.

A: I think you were too friendly to them—that's the problem.

B: I just know that I don't want to fight with them, but I have to do something about this problem!

PROBLEMS AT HOME (pp. 78-79)

Conversation 1: *What's happening?*

A: Mommy, Mommy! Come quick!

B: Just a minute, Stacy.

A: Mommy! The toilet is overflowing!

B: Oh, my goodness! The bathroom is flooded! Where's the plunger?

A: Mommy—here it is, behind the toilet!

B: Stacy, what did you put in the toilet?

A: Nothing, Mommy.

B: Nothing? What's this rubber ducky here? What a day!

Conversation 2: *What's next?*

A: I did my best with these pests. I don't know why you have so many cockroaches!

B: And the mice! This new apartment is a disaster.

A: Well, I sprayed a pesticide around the sink and under the counter. I think that's where the cockroaches are coming from.

B: What should I do about the mice?

A: Don't leave any food around. Try to keep all your food in plastic containers.

B: I know. The mice ate through a box of cereal.

A: And never leave dishes in the sink with food.

B: Yes, I found that out, too. The cockroaches just love my dirty dishes!

UNIT 6: SHOPPING

GOING SHOPPING! (pp. 82-83)

Conversation 1: *What's your opinion?*

A: I love shopping at the mall! It's indoors, so it's always nice weather—cool in summer and warm in winter.

B: Exactly. Like today. It's raining out, but we don't need an umbrella!

A: There are so many shops here—and they all have great buys!

B: It's true. The best stores in town are here—Patterson's Department Store, The Jeans Outlet, that new CD store. . .

A: Yes, and the Bookmark. That bookstore is my favorite place in the mall!

B: My favorite is Munchie's Pet Shop. I always stop there.

A: Really? There's Munchie's now. Do you want to go in?

B: Sure. Oh, look at that cute little white doggie in the window! Isn't she adorable!

Little dog: Yap! Yap!

Conversation 2: *What's happening?*

A: Listen up, kids. You have one hour to shop. We'll meet back here at the mall coffee shop for lunch. One hour! Clear?

B, C: Yeah, yeah. Sure, Mom, one hour.

B: Let's check out the music store; OK, Mike?

C: Sure. Oh, wait a minute—nice weight set. I want that! I'm going to start lifting weights.

B: Yeah? You want to be a body builder, huh?

C: Right. . . Hey, take a look at those speakers! I bet they sound great. Man, they've got everything at that electronics store!

B: Come on, Mike. The music store, remember? I want to see if Loud Metal's new CD is out yet.

C: In a minute, in a minute. . . I really need a new pair of basketball shoes. Let's go back to the sporting goods store.

B: Mike! Let's go!

C: OK, OK. . .

SPORTING GOODS STORE (pp. 84-85)

Conversation 1: *What's next?*

A: May I help you, ma'am?

B: I hope so. My husband watches too much TV—he's a real couch potato. I think he needs a sport. What can I buy him?

A: Well, what sports does he like?

B: All sports. Every weekend he watches sports on TV all day—basketball, football, baseball, hockey, golf. Even soccer and bowling—he watches everything!

A: Hmm. . . Maybe he'd like golf. This nice set of clubs is on sale now. It's a very good price.

B: Oh, my! That's a good price? It's so expensive!

A: In that case, how about this nice starter set? It's not very expensive, and it has all the basic clubs.

B: Oh, that's a good idea! If he likes the set and enjoys playing, he can buy more clubs!

Conversation 2: *What's happening?*

A: You play baseball, don't you, George?

B: Yes, I do. I play every chance I get.

A: Where do you buy your baseball equipment?

B: There's a good sporting goods store downtown, Mickey's Sports. It has all kinds of athletic equipment. And it has pretty good prices, too.

A: Sounds good. My daughter wants to play baseball on a neighborhood team. What will she need?

B: Does she have a glove?

A: No, she's just beginning. She's only seven. She has a baseball cap, but that's all.

B: Well, she'll need a good glove. And maybe a bat and ball. She'll get the uniform with the team. I guess that's about it.

A: You've been a big help. Thanks, George!

TOY TORE (pp. 86-87)

Conversation 1: *What's your opinion?*

A: May I help you, sir?

B: Yes, thanks. My nephew is two years old today. I need to buy something for him.

A: What kinds of toys does he like?

B: I don't know. What do two-year-olds usually like?

A: How about a stuffed animal? We have some really cute ones here—the penguin? that big snake? a teddy bear, maybe?

B: Mmm. . . maybe. This tricycle is nice.

A: Yes, it is.

B: Do you think he might be too young for it? Oh, look at that little boy playing with the truck!

A: He looks about two years old.

B: Yeah, that's a great truck! My nephew will love it! I'll take it!

Conversation 2: *What's next?*

A: OK, kids, I want you to stay right with me! Susie? Where's Susie? Robert, where's your sister?

B: I don't know, Mommy.

A: She was right here a minute ago!

B: There she is, Mommy. She's in the toy store. See? She's playing with that paint set.

A: Oh, my goodness! Playing with a paint set! Hurry up, Robert—stay right with me! I don't want to lose you, too.

B: Oh, now she's pulling the dolls off the shelf! Is Susie a bad girl, Mommy? (*Bump!*)

C: Oh!

A: Oh, I'm sorry, Miss. Are you OK? My three-year-old ran away, and she's in the store here. . .

B: Mommy! Susie's climbed up, and she's playing with the computer! Uh-oh!

A: Oh, no!

SHOE STORE (pp. 88-89)

Conversation 1: *What's your opinion?*

A: Do you have a favorite pair of shoes, Tony?

B: I sure do, May. My old moccasins. They're so comfortable. I wear them all the time at home.

C: I have a pair of shoes like that—my old, suede loafers. I bought them a long time ago, and they fit perfectly. I love them.

D: I'm wearing my favorite shoes today—see?

A, B, C: Wow! Pretty nice! Fancy boots! They're beautiful!

D: They're real Western boots—handmade. I got them in Texas.

A: You all are lucky. I don't have any favorite shoes.

C: You don't?! Why not, May?

A: My shoes never fit right. My feet are wide, and the shoes are always too narrow. As a matter of fact, my feet hurt right now!

Conversation 2: *What's the process?*

A: Let's see, Find Someone Who. . . Brenda, do you have more than ten pairs of shoes?

B: I don't think so, Hiro. How about you?

A: No way! I don't think anybody does. It's a dumb question.

C: What do you mean, "a dumb question"? What's wrong with having more than ten pairs of shoes?

A: More than ten pairs? That's silly! Nobody needs that many shoes!

C: It doesn't seem silly to me.

B: How many pairs of shoes do you have, Molly?

C: Oh, I don't know. . . a few. . .

B: More than ten?

C: I'm not exactly sure how many. Let's see. I have a pair of walking shoes, and running shoes, and loafers, and then shoes for work—gray ones, and blue ones, and, of course, high heels—a black pair, and tan ones, and red ones, and white ones, and some flats, and my sandals, and do boots count? I have black boots, and red boots, and rubber boots. . .

MEN'S CLOTHING STORE (p. 90)

Conversation: *What's the process?*

A: I'm glad you're my partner for this interview, Frank. I don't know anything about shopping for men's clothing.

B: Well, to be honest, Lena, I don't know much about it, either.

A: You don't?! Why not?

B: My wife always buys my clothes for me.

A: Really? What about before you got married?

B: My mother shopped for me. I'm colorblind, so I don't see the colors right. If I buy my clothes, nothing looks good.

A: That's interesting, Frank. But, how can we answer these questions?

B: Why not just write our real answers? I don't think there are any "wrong" answers to these questions, Lena.

WOMEN'S CLOTHING STORE (p. 91)

Conversation: *What's happening?*

A: What's the matter, Jan? You look worried.

B: Oh, I don't know what to do. The party's tomorrow night, and I don't have anything to wear.

A: Why don't you try The Clothes Corner? It's a little dress shop at the shopping mall.

B: I don't think I know it.

A: You don't? Really? Oh, it has everything! Casual wear, sports clothes, bathing suits, hats—and wonderful party dresses!

B: Sounds like the store I need.

A: It's a wonderful store, Jan! Tell you what—let's go to the mall this afternoon. We'll check out The Clothes Corner.

B: And if I don't find anything there, we can look around. There are so many women's clothing stores at the mall.

A: Sure. Don't worry, you'll find something.

DEPARTMENT STORE (pp. 92-93)

Conversation 1: *What's happening?*

A: Can I help you, ma'am?

B: Yes, I need to have this wrapped. The salesclerk said to come over to this counter.

A: That's right. Oh, isn't that a pretty little dress?!

B: It is, isn't it? It's for my granddaughter. We have eight grandsons. Now, finally, a granddaughter! I love to buy dresses for her!

A: Aren't you lucky. Nine grandchildren! What wrapping paper do you prefer?

B: Let's see. . . how about that one with the baby kittens and puppies? That's cute.

A: Good choice. And the ribbon?

B: Oh, pink, of course!

Conversation 2: *What's happening?*

A: Pardon me. Do you know how to get to the home furnishings department?

B: Yes. Take the escalator up to the second floor, then go through the women's department, and it's just past home entertainment.

A: Thanks. Escalator to the second floor, straight ahead through the women's department and home entertainment.

B: Yes, that's right.

A: And the escalator? How do I get to the escalator?

B: The escalator? See the jewelry counter over there? Go around the counter, and it's right on the other side, sir.

A: OK, I see. Thank you.

B: Can I help you with anything else?

A: No, that's all.

FLOWER SHOP (pp. 94-95)

Conversation 1: *What's next?*

A: Yes, sir. Can I help you?

B: I'd like to buy some flowers.

A: For what occasion, sir?

B: Oh, no real occasion. They're for a friend of mine.

A: Is that a woman or a man?

B: A woman.

A: Ah. Are you thinking of a plant or cut flowers?

B: Well, I'm not sure. . . something beautiful. . .

A: A dozen roses, perhaps? We have some very beautiful long-stemmed red roses.

B: That sounds good. Can you deliver them for me?

A: Yes, of course. Would you like a card to write a message?

Conversation 2: *What's your opinion?*

A: Good morning. May I help you?

B: I'd like to get some flowers for Mother's Day.

A: Fine. Do you have anything special in mind? A corsage, maybe?

B: Yes, that would be nice. We're going to take Mother out to dinner, and she could wear the corsage then. What kind of flower would you suggest?

A: A gardenia, perhaps?

B: Oh, I love gardenias. They smell wonderful. But my mother doesn't like them.

A: How about an orchid? We have orchid corsages already made up.

B: I'm afraid my mother doesn't like orchids, either. You know, maybe a floral arrangement is better.

A: A bouquet of spring flowers in a pretty vase?

B: That sounds wonderful! I know my mother will like that!

PHARMACY (pp. 96-97)

Conversation 1: *What's next?*

A: Excuse me.

B: Yes, sir. May I help you?

A: Oh, I hope so. I have a terrible cold. I can't breathe. I can't sleep. I need something strong!

B: Well, we have some Stuffy's cold medicine.

A: I just saw that on TV. How is it?

B: Well, I usually take Get Well cold medicine when I get sick, but I'm afraid we're all sold out. I hear, though, that Stuffy's is very good.

A: I guess I'll try it, then.

B: Stuffy's will make you very sleepy, so don't take it before you drive.

A: Don't worry. I'm not going anywhere—except to bed!

Conversation 2: *What's the process?*

A: I don't understand this Community Activity very well, Merle.

B: What don't you understand about it, Amy?

A: I'm not sure. . . I just don't know what to do.

B: Well, we have to go to two different stores.

A: Two pharmacies or just two stores? I buy all these things at the supermarket.

B: Hmm. . . you're right. I guess the supermarket can be one of the stores.

A: OK, good. And we look for only one brand and one size of each item, right?

B: That's right. The same brand and the same size at both stores.

A: OK. I don't understand "dose." What does that mean?

B: Where's that? Oh, I see. The dose is the amount in each tablet or capsule. It's in milligrams. Like, 500 milligrams.

A: I understand. This won't be hard. I can do this activity and my supermarket shopping at the same time!

JEWELRY STORE (p. 98)

Conversation: *What happened?*

A: I guess we're partners for this interview, Barbara.

B: Oh, good! Now I can ask you about that beautiful ring you're wearing, Izumi.

A: It's new. You like it?

B: I love it! It's gold, isn't it?

A: Uh-huh.

B: And the beautiful green stone—what is it?

A: It's an emerald.

B: It's just wonderful! If you don't mind my asking, was it a present?

A: Yes. My boyfriend gave it to me last night. We've been going together for a year, so it's kind of an anniversary present.

B: Wow! What a wonderful boyfriend! He has good taste in jewelry, Izumi!

HARDWARE STORE (p. 99)

Conversation: *What's next?*

A: What hardware store do you go to, Sam?

B: I always shop at Sullivan's. It's so big, you can find anything you want there. And they have the lowest prices in town. I got a great deal on my power saw there!

A: I like Brace Hardware better. They're friendlier. And they have so many brands of paint.

C: I never go to the hardware store. I don't do any repairs around the house. I'm just not handy.

D: Me, too. I'm all thumbs. I always hit my thumb when I try to hammer a nail.

B: Who does your household repairs?
D: Nobody. Would *you* like to, Sam?
C: Hey, good idea! Can you do my repairs, too, Sam?
B: Uh. . . well. . . I don't know. . .

OFFICE SUPPLY STORE (p. 100)

Conversation: *What's your opinion?*

A: Can you type, Babbu?
B: Yes, I can, Sara. Can you?
A: No, I can't. Can you change a typewriter ribbon?
B: No. I never use a typewriter. I type on a word processor. I can change an ink cartridge on a printer. Does that count?
A: I think that's different.
B: Yeah, I guess so. Do you use computers at all, Sara?
A: No, but next semester I'm going to take a basic computer course.
B: That's a good idea. These days, everybody needs to know how to use a computer.

ELECTRONICS STORE (p. 101)

Conversation: *What's your opinion?*

A: The trouble with electronic equipment is that when you buy it, it's already outdated.
B: You're right. Every day there's something new. It's impossible to keep up.
C: That's so true. I bought a really nice tape deck a few years ago. But now everybody has CDs.
B: Yeah, a small CD player doesn't cost very much now.
C: I know, but I have hundreds of tapes, and I can't use them with a CD player!
A: I know what you mean. I had the same problem with my computer.
D: Well, I don't worry about it. My little old black & white TV is just fine for me.
A, B, C: You don't have a color TV? You're kidding!

SALES AND ADVERTISEMENTS (pp. 102-103)

Conversation 1: *What happened?*

A: We had a yard sale last spring.
B: Really? What did you sell?
A: Well, first we cleaned the whole house. Then we put everything we didn't want in the yard sale.
C: Where did you have it, Cecilia?
A: In front of our apartment building. We don't have a yard, so it was really a sidewalk sale.
B: Did many people come?
A: Oh, yes. We were busy all day. The hard part was putting prices on everything. The rest was pretty easy.
C: Will you do it again?
A: I don't know. Maybe when we clean the whole house again. But we'll be more careful next time. Last spring we sold my favorite sweater by mistake!

Conversation 2: *What's the process?*

A: Did you bring an ad for sales, Sung?
B: No, I didn't. I was busy at work, and I forgot all about it.
C: I didn't bring one, either. I remembered, but I

couldn't find one.
D: That's OK. I brought a few ads with me. We can all look at mine.
A, B, C: That's great, Mia! Thanks a lot. All right!
A: Where'd you find so many, Mia?
D: Oh, the Sunday newspaper always has lots of sale ads in it.
C: Hey, look at this! A white sale, and I need new sheets! Thanks, Mia!

UNIT 7: COMMUNITY

YOUR NEIGHBORHOOD (pp. 106-107)

Conversation 1: *What's happening?*

A: What kind of neighborhood do you live in now, Andy?
B: It's a very busy neighborhood. There are lots of stores: a newspaper store, a pizza shop, a shoemaker, a bakery, and a fruit store.
A: My neighborhood is more residential. There's a convenience store, but that's it.
B: Have you lived there a long time?
A: I sure have! I grew up in the neighborhood. When my parents moved to the suburbs, I stayed.
B: I just moved into my neighborhood. I think I'll like it. You must like where you live.
A: Absolutely. It's a nice place. I know everyone, even the mailman and the ice cream man. The ice cream truck comes in the afternoon just like when I was a kid!
B: I love ice cream. Too bad the ice cream truck doesn't come to my neighborhood!

Conversation 2: *What's next?*

A: What's good about your neighborhood, Selena?
B: Well, my neighbors are great. They're very helpful. How about yours?
A: In my neighborhood, the street is very clean. Everyone is very careful with their trash. And the recycling bins are always full.
B: What's bad about your neighborhood?
A: Let's see. . . there aren't enough parking spaces, and the street corner is dangerous. There are always accidents there.
B: Is there a traffic light there?
A: No, but we need one. There's a lot of traffic all the time.
B: Why don't you and your neighbors write a petition?

YOUR COMMUNITY (pp. 108-109)

Conversation 1: *What's happening?*

A: It's great to be in New York!

B: It sure is! Hey, do you know how to get to the theater?

A: No, do you?

B: Nope. Why don't we ask someone?

A: Good idea. . . Excuse me. Could you tell us where the Royal Theater is?

C: Sure. See this street? Go straight for three blocks. You'll see a parking lot on the left. At that corner, turn left. Go one block and the theater is just before the corner, next to a Japanese restaurant.

B: Let's see. We walk three blocks and turn left at the parking lot. Then we go one block, and the Royal Theater is just before the corner, right?

C: Exactly. Enjoy the show!

A, B: Thanks a lot. Thanks.

Conversation 2: *What's next?*

A: Are you sure you know how to get to the Statue of Liberty?

B: Of course! We just keep walking down Broadway.

A: Well, we've been walking for an hour. Let's just ask someone.

B: I'm telling you—it's right behind the Chrysler Building, near the Empire State Building.

A: I'm going to ask this woman, anyway. Excuse me, miss. We're looking for the Statue of Liberty.

C: Well, you have a long way to go. Take the subway to South Ferry. Then you have to take the ferry to get to the statue. The Statue of Liberty is across from South Ferry.

A: Thanks very much.

C: No problem. Oh, and Ellis Island is close to the statue. You should see that, too. Same ferry.

A: Great. Thanks again. By the way, where is the subway?

THE TELEPHONE (pp. 110-111)

Conversation 1: *What's happening?*

(telephone conversation)

A: Hello. Can I please speak to Mary? This is Susan.

B: I'm sorry. She's not home right now. Can I take a message?

A: Yes. I'm from her class. My name is Susan Gomez.

B: Could you spell your last name, please?

A: Sure: G-o-m-e-z. Please ask her to call me. My number is 555-6784.

B: OK. Let me repeat that. Susan Gomez, 555-6785. Please call.

A: Actually, it's 6784.

B: Oh, sorry.

A: That's OK. Thanks. Bye-bye.

B: Bye.

Conversation 2: *What's happening?*

(telephone conversation)

A: Good morning. English Language Center. Can I help you?

B: Yes. This is Raymond Liu. I can't come to school today.

A: Just a minute. I'll connect you to the teachers' room.

C: Good morning. Teachers' room.

B: Hello. Is Mr. Park there?

C: Yes. Just a moment, please.

Teacher: Hello?

B: Hi, Mr. Park. It's Raymond. I can't come to school today. I'm sick.

Teacher: I'm sorry to hear that, Raymond. I hope you feel better. See you soon, OK? Take care!

B: Thanks. I hope I'll be back next week. Bye.

EMERGENCY: FIRE! (pp. 112-113)

Conversation 1: *What's next?*

A: Oh, no! Look! A fire downstairs in the trash!

B: Let's call the fire department.

A: What's the number? I can't remember!

B: Here it is—we wrote it next to the telephone. . .

C: Hello. Fire Department.

B: Yes. We want to report a fire. It's in the trash near our building—5034 River Street.

C: OK. What's your name and telephone number, sir?

B: Sam Kim. 555-0928. And, please hurry! It looks like it's getting worse!

C: We'll send the fire engine right away.

Conversation 2: *What's happening?*

Reporter: I'm on the scene of a large fire at the corner of River Street and Fifth. Looks like a small trash fire burned out of control due to strong winds. The flames quickly engulfed the apartment building at 5034 River Street. Thankfully, everyone made it safely outside. Wait—I see an elderly man on a stretcher. The EMT team is putting him in the ambulance. Here's Fire Chief Ryan. Chief Ryan, what happened?

Fire Chief: We arrived on the scene within minutes of the call. But the windy conditions were very difficult. We were lucky to get everyone out of the building. One man was rescued from the first floor. He's going to be OK, but the ambulance is taking him to the hospital. The firefighters are very tired now. One or two are suffering from smoke inhalation.

Reporter: Thanks, Chief Ryan. Back to you, Chuck, at the news desk.

EMERGENCY: POLICE! (pp. 114-115)

Conversation 1: *What's next?*

(telephone conversation)

A: Hi, Steve! Wait till I tell you what happened today!

B: What?

A: Well, I was studying when I heard a noise outside. Two guys were breaking into my car! I ran to the phone and called the police.

B: Oh, no! What happened next?

A: The police came immediately. The sirens were so loud. The guys tried to run away, but. . .

B: Did the police catch them?

A: One officer yelled, "Freeze!" and they stopped in their tracks. The police put handcuffs on them, read them their rights, and arrested them.

B: Is there any damage to your car?

A: Gee, I was so upset, I didn't look. I'll go and check now. Thanks, Steve.

Conversation 2: *What happened?*

A: Hi, Christina. I've been worried. Why are you so late?

B: Well, when I finished shopping at the mall, I went out to the parking lot, and my car wasn't there!

A: What did you do?

B: I found the mall security police.

A: Did they help you?

B: The officer took down the information about the car— I described it and told him where I parked.

A: What happened next?

B: He suggested we ride around the parking lot and look for it. But I told him I knew where it was, and it wasn't there.

A: So tell me, what happened?

B: Well, the car *was* there, exactly where I parked it—in a completely different spot from where I thought. I was so embarrassed!

THE POST OFFICE (pp. 116-117)

Conversation 1: *What's the process?*

Teacher: Let's practice taking notes today. Gino, you be the teacher.

A: OK. Class, open your notebooks to the Class Activities section. What headings do we write?

B: "Customers" and "Postal Workers." I'll write it on the board.

A: OK. What's the first question? Oh, there's only one: What is happening in the picture?

C: One customer is mailing a letter. Write that in the "Customers" column?

A: Yes. Write "mailing a letter." What else?

D: One is weighing a package.

A: Where does that go?

D: In the "Customers" column.

A: No, the *postal worker* is weighing the package. It goes in the "Postal Workers" column!

Conversation 2: *What's next?*

A: Good morning. My, you have a lot of packages! Just put them on the counter here.

B: Thanks. Yes, most of my family lives far away.

A: OK, where should we start?

B: These. Send them by overnight mail, please. They have to arrive tomorrow.

A: Let's see how much they weigh. . . OK, what's next?

B: These here—they can go parcel post.

A: All right. They're heavy, too. It'll be much cheaper sending them parcel post.

B: And these.

A: Where are they going?

B: Oh, these are international mail. They'll go air mail.

A: Anything else?

THE BANK (pp. 118-119)

Conversation 1: *What's happening?*

A: Good morning, sir. How can I help you?

B: I'd like to cash my paycheck, please.

A: Do you have your bank card?

B: Yes, here it is.

A: Please punch in your personal identification number. Then press "end."

B: (*to himself*) Hmm. Is it my birthday? My address? Oh, yes! It's the last four digits of my phone number. . .

A: Here you are, sir.

B: Thanks. . . One hundred fifty-one. One hundred fifty-two. Excuse me. I think there's a mistake. My check was for one hundred sixty-seven.

A: Let me see. . . Oh my goodness, you're right. I'm so sorry!

Conversation 2: *What's happening?*

A: Good afternoon. How can I help you?

B: Hi. I'd like to straighten out my checking account. I think it's overdrawn.

A: All right. What's your account number?

B: 219124456.

A: Let's see. . . Oh. Looks like there's a small problem. I think you didn't subtract the service fee.

B: Oh, how careless! I subtract the fee every month. I guess I forgot this time. Well, I'd like to transfer funds from my savings account.

A: OK. Here's a withdrawal slip and a deposit slip to fill out.

B: This is so embarrassing!

A: No problem.

PUBLIC TRANSPORTATION (pp. 120-121)

Conversation 1: *What's happening?*

A: Excuse me. Can you tell me which train to take to get to Hudson Station?

B: Take the Green Line. Get off at Park Street; go downstairs and transfer to the Red Line. Hudson Station is the last stop.

A: I'm not sure I understand. Where do I get the Green Line?

B: First, buy a token. The fare is $1.50. Then go through that turnstile. Get on the train that says "Green Line." Then ride one, two, three stops to Park Street. Be sure to get on the train marked Hudson Station. Got it?

A: OK. The Green Line to Park Street. Transfer to the Red Line to Hudson Station. Where's the platform for the Red Line?

B: It's downstairs at Park Street. Remember to go downstairs. Get on the rear of the train. The staircase will be right there when you get off at Park.

A: Thanks. You've been very patient.

B: No problem. Glad to help.

Conversation 2: *What's the process?*

A: Let's get this Group Survey done before the bell rings. We never seem to finish!

B: OK. I'll be the recorder. What are the advantages of bus transportation?

C: Well, it's cheap. It's the cheapest form of transportation.

A: No, it's not. Your feet are cheaper!

C: Oops! You're right! But feet aren't as fast.

B: Then we won't check the "fast" box for feet, but let's check "cheap."

A: Let's get back to bus transportation. What about convenient?

D: Yup—the bus is convenient. There's a bus stop at my corner.

A, B, C: I agree. That's right. Sure.

C: How about fast? Is the bus fast?

A, B, D: No way! It's too slow. Sure, it's fast—like a turtle!

(*Bell rings.*)

B: Darn—the bell! We never finish!

YOUR CAR (p. 122)

Conversation: *What's next?*

A: Guess what! I just bought a car!

B: You did! Congratulations, Ken!

A: Do you want to see it? I drove it to school today.

B: We have 15 minutes before class begins. Let's go!

(*a few minutes later*)

A: Isn't it beautiful! Brand new paint job, new brakes, new clutch.

B: Oh, look—you have a vanity plate! Your license says "KENZCAR"! That's cute!

A: Want to go for a quick ride around the parking lot?

(*They go for a ride.*)

B: Ken, this is great. But why is it making so much noise?

A: Uh-oh, sounds like the muffler. Well, I guess not everything is new!

TRAFFIC AND ROAD SIGNS (p. 123)

Conversation: *What's happening?*

A: Some of the signs on the road still confuse us. Would you help us review them?

Teacher: Sure, I'd be glad to. Let's start with an easy one—red and octagon. Without even reading the word, what is it?

A: I know that one. "STOP." What about this one? "YIELD." What does it mean?

Teacher: Yield signs are always upside down triangles. "Yield" means to give the other driver the right of way. They're always at intersections. Now what do all yellow signs indicate?

B: I know that from my driving test. . . caution, slow down. A lot of them have pictures: like schoolchildren and pedestrians.

Teacher: You both know a lot! How about white signs?

A: You have to take certain precautions: for example, slippery pavements or no bicycles.

Teacher: I can't think of anything else to ask. You are wise to review these signs. You can drive with confidence now!

THE GAS STATION (p. 124)

Conversation: *What's next?*

A: I think I'd better stop for gas, Betty.

B: Here's a gas station, Ken. Let's pull in.

A: Oh, good—it's a self-service station. That saves me some money. I always take premium gasoline, and it's more expensive.

B: If you pump the gas, I'll check the oil, OK?

A: How do you know how to check the oil?

B: My father taught me. He said it's a good thing to learn. I can change a tire, too!

A: I'm impressed. Most women don't know how to do that. . .

B: Ken, you need water in the radiator!

A: How do you know *that*?

THE LAUNDROMAT AND DRY CLEANERS (p. 125)

Conversation: *What's happening?*

TV Housewife: Just look at these dirty clothes! Stains everywhere! Bleaching doesn't get the stains out. How will they ever get clean?

Narrator: Washo detergent gets the dirt out! Just use Washo once and see the difference: Your whites will be whiter! Your colors will be brighter. . . Just put Washo in your wash cycle and presto! Fresh and clean! White wash, dark wash, any wash!

TV Housewife: I always had problems with my laundry until Washo came along. I put Washo in the wash cycle, press the cold water button, and, at the end of the rinse cycle, my clothes are fresh and clean. They even *smell* cleaner. Thank you, Washo!

UNIT 8: WORK

WORK EVERYONE DOES! (pp. 128-129)

Conversation 1: *What's happening?*

A: I hate to do housework! It never ends.

B: Come on. Let's do it together. Two can do it in half the time!

A: But there is so much to do, I don't know where to start!

B: Let's make a list. What's most important today?

A: Definitely dusting the furniture, vacuuming, washing the windows. . .

B: OK. I'll wash the windows, and you can dust and vacuum. What's next?

A: Let's see. . . Cleaning the refrigerator, defrosting the freezer, changing the burned-out light bulbs. I don't know where to begin!

B: Maria, just do some today, and then some next time. Don't worry about finishing it all today.

A: Oh, Paco. Thanks so much for coming over to help me.

B: No problem. It's fun when we do things together, Maria!

Conversation 2: *What's the process?*

A: A new class game—"Test Your Memory"—looks like fun!

B: I'm not sure how to do it.

A: It's easy. But you have to concentrate! Just listen to the teacher.

Teacher: OK, class. Close your books.

C: What do we do now?

Teacher: Try to clear your minds and concentrate. I'll tell a story. Just listen and remember. Then open your books and write the correct order of the events in the boxes.

C: Can we take notes?

Teacher: No, this is practice in listening. Listen and pay attention to the sequence of the activities. Then write the correct order. When you are done, we'll read the story together. OK, ready?

HOME REPAIRS (pp. 130-131)

Conversation 1: *What's happening?*

A: What happened to the lights?

B: Don't worry. It's probably just the circuit breaker. Where's the flashlight?

A: I'm in the middle of sewing this costume for the Halloween party! How will I get this done by tomorrow?

B: Don't worry. You can get back to the sewing machine as soon as I flip the circuit breaker. Do you know where the flashlight is?

A: It's in the kitchen—in the drawer next to the stove. Oh, no! I dropped the thread and scissors and now I can't find them!

B: Just a minute. I'll be right back.

A: Could you please hurry? I really have to get this costume done tonight!

Conversation 2: *What happened?*

A: Hi. What are you writing about in your journal, Cosmo?

B: Well, the lesson is about home repairs, so I'm writing about the time I was hanging a door and the hinge broke.

A: The hinge broke! How did that happen?

B: I was attaching the hinge and my daughter tried to open the door.

A: Oh, no! Why did she do that?

B: She's only three. She didn't know any better.

A: Did you get hurt?

B: No, but the door almost fell on my daughter! It was pretty scary!

JOBS (pp. 132-133)

Conversation 1: *What's your opinion?*

A: Hmm. I'm not sure about this last picture.

B: You mean, Number 4? The man's cutting trees. He's a tree cutter.

C: My dictionary says that's a "woodcutter."

D: Mine says a "lumberjack."

A: Yes, but look at the trees. They're Christmas trees.

D: Maybe he's a Christmas tree cutter.

B: Is that a job?

C: I think he's on a tree farm. He's a tree farmer.

D: Maybe he's a Christmas tree farmer!

Conversation 2: *What's the process?*

A: Good evening, ladies and gentlemen. We are happy to have with us Mr. Rocky Road, the famous rock star. Hi, Rocky! Thanks for joining us.

B: Good evening, Jay. Hello, everyone. . .

A: Does anyone in the audience want to ask Rocky a question?

C: Oh, Mr. Road. . . It's so nice to meet you. I'm Wanda Lee. Where do you work?

B: Where do I work? The world is my theater. I work in theaters around the world.

D: Mr. Road, what hours do you work?

B: I work long hours. My band and I practice for many weeks before our concert tours. Sometimes our concerts are two hours long!

A: OK, one more question. Yes, the young lady in the pink dress.

E: Um-um-um, Rocky, do you like your job?

B: Wait, this is too silly! Is this role play over yet?

CLOTHING FOR WORK (pp. 134-135)

Conversation 1: *What's happening?*

A: I just got a new job—I'm working in a lab!

B: Congratulations! What's your job?

A: I'm a lab technician. I do lab tests and write up results.

B: Sounds great. Do you have to wear a uniform?

A: Yes, I wear a lab coat. It's white and has big pockets. I have a name tag on my coat.

B: I bet you look like a scientist! Hey, who pays for the coat? Do you have to buy it?

A: Good question. I think the company pays for it.

B: Well, good luck on your new job. It sounds great!

Conversation 2: *What's happening?*

A: Your police officer's uniform is so impressive! Pockets everywhere, matching pants and shirt.

B: Thanks. I like the hat best. I think it's very official.

A: Are you worried about carrying a gun and nightstick?

B: Not really. I learned how to be careful when I was at the academy. What do *you* wear at work?

A: You'll never guess, but try.

B: Do you wear a uniform?

A: No. Guess again.

B: A special shirt?

A: No.

B: An everyday shirt?

A: No—no shirt, actually.

B: No shirt?

A: No—and no pants.

B: No pants?! Do you wear shoes?

A: No.

B: Well, what *do* you wear?

A: I'm a lifeguard. I wear a bathing suit and a whistle!

Conversation 1: *What happened?*

A: Guess what happened at work today! The safety inspector visited us!

B: What happened?

A: Well, it was terrible! We had several violations.

B: What are violations?

A: They are things we do that are not safe. They are against the rules.

B: Like what?

A: Well, no one was wearing safety glasses or safety gloves on the assembly line. That's a violation, and it's dangerous.

B: Are there warning signs in the factory?

A: Yes, but no one pays attention to the signs! The foreman and the supervisor were very embarrassed.

Conversation 2: *What's the process?*

A: Good thing it's time for a break. I'm tired!

B: Me, too. Feels good to take off this hard hat for a few minutes.

C: Oh, hi, Chris. How is your first day going?

D: It's OK, but I'm confused by some of the signs. Like, what does "AUTHORIZED PERSONNEL" mean?

A: That means that we can't go in—only people who have permission can enter. Can I help you with anything else?

D: Yeah! What is "HIGH VOLTAGE"?

C: "High Voltage" means that there is so much electricity it's dangerous. Be careful around high voltage!

D: Well, break's over. Time to put my mask on and get back to spraying! Thanks for your help.

C: Sure. See you later.

A: What a nice guy! I'm going to enjoy working with him.

B: Yeah, me, too.

Conversation 1: *What's next?*

A: Miki, what a great idea. A ride in the country with you makes a perfect Sunday.

B: I love seeing all the farms here. Look at the cows over there. Oh, and look—a baby cow!

A: That's a calf, Miki. Look at all the barnyard animals. Looks like the animals all had babies—look at the hens and chicks near the chicken coop!

B: And the ducks and ducklings. What funny noises they make!

A: There's the pig and her babies at the trough. They must be thirsty!

B: Yoshi, I think the mother pig is called a sow, and the babies are piglets, right?

A: Um, yes. That's what I meant.

B: Yoshi, let's come back in the fall and pick apples. That would be fun!

Conversation 2: *What's happening?*

A: Man, it's hot today. And we have so much more work to do.

B: Did you finish milking the cows?

A: A long time ago. The milking machine makes it easy, but Clarabell doesn't know what it is. She's used to the old fashioned way. How about the sheep?

B: Yeah, I just finished shearing the sheep. They didn't like it at all.

A: They were just nervous. It doesn't hurt with all that wool!

B: What are we going to do this afternoon?

A: Plenty. We have to feed hay to the horses. Then, we have to get the field ready for planting with the tractor.

B: Hey, who are those city slickers over there? I bet they don't know the difference between a cow and a bull!

A: I don't think they care. Look at them. They're in love!

Conversation 1: *What's happening?*

A: Well, Frank, you finally decided to come to work! You're an hour late!

B: Sorry, Mr. Jones. It won't happen again.

A: I certainly hope not! The meeting was at 8:00. Did you forget?

B: No. My wife is sick, and. . .

A: I'm not interested in excuses, Frank! We all have problems.

B: Yes, I understand that. It's just. . .

A: Just don't let it happen again.

B: Right. Uh. . . It won't, Mr. Jones. Don't worry.

Conversation 2: *What happened?*

A: How was your first day of work?

B: Oh, it was terrible! I was so embarrassed!

A: I'm sorry to hear that. Tell me about it.

B: Well, first of all, the job is great. It's just what I wanted. And the personnel officer was friendly and helpful.

A: Sounds great. What went wrong?

B: When I came into the office, everyone was staring! They all wear casual clothes—very casual—jeans and T-shirts. And there I was in a *suit*!

A: But it was your first day. I'm sure they understood. You felt self-conscious, that's all!

B: Did I ever! I wanted to run away! I couldn't do anything at my desk.

A: Hey, I have an idea. Let's go shopping for some new jeans. That will make you feel better!

Conversation 1: *What's the process?*

A: It's been a while since we've done a Group Activity. Let's do this one together.

B: OK. It'll be you, me, and Liz. Now, first question: What are good reasons to quit a job?

A: Let's see. . . I know! Poor performance.

C: What does that mean? Isn't poor the opposite of rich?

A: Not in this case! It means "bad."

B: That's not quitting a job. That's getting fired!

A: Oops! You're right! Quitting. . . Let's see. . .

C: Better job opportunity somewhere else!
(Bell rings.)

B: Again we didn't finish! I wonder if we'll ever finish an activity!

Conversation 2: *What happened?*

A: You look upset. What's wrong?

B: Oh, nothing. Well. . . Yes, something. I just lost my job!

A: Oh, no! That's terrible! What happened?

B: Well, I worked in the typewriter factory in town. You know, I worked there for 15 years. Now the factory just closed down and is moving outside the country! We *all* lost our jobs!

A: That's awful. What will you do?

B: I don't know. I can collect unemployment for a while. But as far as a job, there aren't many opportunities here. That factory employed hundreds of people!

A: Why don't you think about going back to school?

B: That's a good idea. I need to learn more about modern technology. Maybe I can learn about computers!

FINDING A JOB (pp. 144-145)

Conversation 1: *What's next?*

A: I really need to get a job; I don't even know where to start looking.

B: There are so many ways to start. Why don't you ask around?

A: I did. No one has any jobs. I even checked the bulletin boards at school!

B: How about the want ads in the newspaper? Those ads always have lots of jobs! Look in the paper here.

A: Thanks. Hmm. . . Let's see. . . Here's one I'd be interested in. A truck loader. Yeah, I could do that. I'm strong.

B: You could work part time until the semester is over, then work full time this summer.

A: Oh, wait. It says you should be willing to work all three shifts. I can't do that. I have class in the morning.

B: Well, check it out, anyway. You have to apply in person. Explain your situation. Maybe they'll understand.

A: Great idea.

B: Well, good luck. Let me know how things go!

Conversation 2: *What's the process?*

A: Good morning, Cecilia. It's nice to meet you. Come right in.

B: Thank you, Mr. Gold. Thanks for seeing me.

A: Let me tell you a little about this job, Cecilia. You would be my secretary. There is a lot of organization work—you know, filing and keeping track of different projects.

B: I have a lot of experience doing that, Mr. Gold. I work in the foreign student office at the college. I file and organize projects for my supervisor.

A: What kind of projects do you work on?

B: Well, we keep track of the students' visas. Often, we have to correspond with the foreign university where the students studied before.

A: That sounds interesting. Why do you want to leave that job?

B: Well, it's a part-time job. I don't make much money. And I'm graduating in May.

A: Let me tell you some other things about this job. . .

BENEFITS (pp. 146-147)

Conversation 1: *What's happening?*

A: I think I got the job as Mr. Gold's secretary, Mom!

B: Great! I'm very proud of you. Did you discuss salary?

A: Oh. . . I was too nervous to bring that up!

B: That's OK. I'm sure they will call you with an offer. Did you discuss benefits?

A: No. Why do I need benefits? What *are* benefits, anyway?

B: They are company-paid expenses, like vacation; they pay you on vacation even though you aren't working. That's a benefit. And health insurance.

A: My part-time job didn't give me those things. Do you only get benefits for full-time work?

B: Usually. Benefits are valuable; they are worth about twenty percent of your salary!

A: Wow! Really?

Conversation 2: *What's the process?*

A: We only have ten minutes to do this Group Discussion activity. Let's try to finish this time, please!

B: OK, let's get started.

A: And let's stick to the topic. We always talk about other things and we never finish!

B: Right! First question: When do you take a sick day?

C: I hardly take sick days. I don't get paid for sick days.

A: I never take sick days. I'm never sick.

B: Sometimes I call in sick when I'm sick of work. I work 40 hours a week and go to school full time, too. Occasionally, I just take a day off.

C: You do? What happens?

B: Nothing. I just stay home and relax. Then I go back to work the next day.

A: Doesn't anyone find out?

B: No, and please don't tell anyone! It's a secret.
(Bell rings.)

A: Darn—the bell! We didn't finish again. We only did one question. We're getting worse!

UNIT 9: HEALTH

THE BODY (pp. 150-151)

Conversation 1: *What's next?*

A: My body is really out of shape. I need to exercise.

B: Why don't you join our exercise class, Mo? It's fun.

A: What do you do?

C: Aerobics. The instructor is very good.

B: Yes. She gives us a real workout!

C: Man, that's the truth! At the end of the class, I ache all over, from my head to my toes.

A: Well, I don't know. . .

B: Oh, come on, Mo. Try it. It's a great way to get in shape!

Conversation 2: *What's the process?*

A: A Group Game! Ted, you be the leader this time.

B: OK. Give me a minute. . . I'm thinking. . . OK, I'm ready.

C: Is it at the top of your body?

B: No, it isn't.

C: Is it at the bottom?

B: Nope. It's not at the bottom.

A: In the middle?

B: No, not in the middle, either.

C: Hmm. . . Is it part of your legs?

B: Yes, it is.

C: I know what it is! Is it your knees?

B: You guessed it! Now you're the leader, Jenny.

STAYING HEALTHY (pp. 152-153)

Conversation 1: *What's happening?*

A: Looks like today will be a busy day at the clinic, Clara.

B: I know. It's only 10:30, and we have a room full of patients.

A: Yes, a lot of checkups today. Most of them are healthy, thank goodness.

B: Wasn't that baby cute? It was fun to measure him and weigh him. He's grown a lot since he was here last month!

A: He sure has! And he's up to date on his vaccinations. His mother is really careful about that.

B: Yes. She was here every month for a checkup when she was pregnant.

A: Oh, I remember. She needed a cholesterol check every month, too, right?

B: Yes. But she's doing great. She eats well and controls her high cholesterol with a good diet. She's really smart. Uh-oh. . . Here we go again—more patients!

Conversation 2: *What's the process?*

A: This Group Activity should be interesting. I want to know how you guys stay healthy! It's so hard with all the junk food around these days!

B: That's true, but it's still important to eat healthy! What do you think is a healthy meal, Insu?

C: I eat a lot of rice and fish. But I don't eat vegetables—I hate vegetables!

A: That's funny. I eat a lot of vegetables, but I don't like fish. I'm a vegetarian.

B: Paco, you also like to eat pasta, remember?

A: Yes. I like pasta, especially before I ride my bike a long distance. It gives me energy!

C: What kinds of exercise does everyone else do?

B: I don't exercise much. I'd like to, but I'm too busy. Does anyone else have that problem?

GETTING SICK (pp. 154-155)

Conversation 1: *What's next?*

A: Oh. . . I feel sick.

B: What's the matter, Jodi?

A: I don't know. I'm dizzy and nauseous. . . and my stomach feels awful.

B: Maybe it's something you ate.

A: I don't think so. I wasn't hungry today, so I didn't eat much. Just some toast and tea.

B: I don't think toast and tea could make you sick.

A: No, I don't think so, either. I have a headache, too, and my neck is stiff. . . and I feel kind of hot!

B: I think you need to go to bed right now. It sounds like the flu!

Conversation 2: *What's your opinion?*

A: What do you have in your medicine cabinet, Peter?

B: Oh, lots of things! Let's see. . . I have headache tablets; ibuprofen for pain; antacid tablets for a stomachache; cold medicine; and cough medicine.

A: Wow! That *is* a lot!

B: That's not all. Nasal spray for a stuffy nose; anti-diarrhea medicine. . . I know there's more, but I forget the rest.

A: Why do you have so many medicines?

B: In case I get sick. Then I can take something right away and feel better fast. What do you have in your medicine cabinet, Steve?

A: Well, not much. I have some aspirin, but I never take it. To be honest, I never get sick, so I don't need medicine.

B: Lucky you!

GOING TO A DOCTOR (pp. 156-157)

Conversation 1: *What's the process?*

(telephone conversation)

A: Dr. Harris' office.

B: This is Ken Lee calling. I'd like to make an appointment for an eye exam.

A: Have you seen the doctor before?

B: No, I haven't. I'm a new patient.

A: All right. How about next Tuesday afternoon at 3:30?

B: That'll be fine.

A: Do you have insurance, Mr. Lee?

B: Yes, I do. I'm on the state plan.

A: Fine. You'll need to bring your insurance card. That's next Tuesday, August 12, at 3:30.

B: Got it. Thanks.

Conversation 2: *What's happening?*

A: Hello, I'm Dr. Johnson. How are you today, Mrs. Brown?

B: Just fine, Doctor.

A: Let's see now. . . Hmm. . . What did you come in for today, Mrs. Brown? It doesn't say on the form.

B: It doesn't? Oh, I guess I forgot to fill it in. Sorry.

A: That's OK. Are you having any problems?

B: No. . . Wait, I did have a problem. Of course. I wrote it down right here. Let's see, where did I put that note. . . Maybe in my purse. . . Oh, dear. . . I can't seem to find it.

A: That's OK. Take your time.

B: Here it is! Yes, of course. I do have a problem, Dr. Johnson. I can't remember anything!

MEDICAL EMERGENCIES (pp. 158-159)

Conversation 1: *What happened?*

A: Wow, that's a big cast on your arm. What happened to you, Jimmy?

B: I broke my arm.

A: How did you do that?

B: Skateboarding.

A: What happened?

B: Well, you know my dog, Sisko? I was skateboarding, and Sisko was running along beside me the way he always does. . .

A: Yeah. . .

B: All of a sudden, a cat ran out in front of me, and Sisko started to chase the cat, and the cat jumped on the skateboard, and then Sisko jumped on me!

A: Oh, no!

B: And then I was on the ground, and Sisko and the cat and the skateboard were all on top of me. I guess I fell on my arm, 'cause it's broken.

A: Wow! I bet that hurts!

Conversation 2: *What's next?*

A: Next stop, Farnham Heights.

B: Ah. . . (*falls down*)

Passengers: Oh, my goodness! What happened? What's going on? What's wrong? Somebody fainted! It's a heart attack!

C: Stand back! Give him some room!

D: Stop the bus! Driver, stop the bus!

E: I'm an EMT. Please stand back, everybody.

B: Mmm. . . Oh. . . What. . . What happened?

E: It's all right. You fainted. How're you feeling now?

HOSPITAL (pp. 160-161)

Conversation 1: *What's the process?*

A: OK, we have to write a story about the hospital scene on this page. Two sentences from everybody. Who's first?

B: Do we have to write about the whole scene? Can our story be just a part of the scene?

C: You mean like, just one patient?

B: Yes. Like the woman with the broken leg, or the man who's sleeping.

C: Sleeping?! He looks like he's dying!

D: Which one? I see two men with their eyes closed.

B: So, what do you think? Do we have to write about everything?

D: Maybe we should ask the teacher.

A: No, we can just decide ourselves. I think we can do it either way. Which way do you prefer?

Conversation 2: *What's happening?*

A: Are you looking for something?

B: Yes, I'm a little lost here.

A: Where do you want to go?

B: I'm supposed to get a chest X-ray.

A: Have you checked in at the Outpatient desk yet?

B: No. Do I go there first?

A: Yes. They'll do the paperwork there. Then they'll send you down to X-ray. I'll take you over to Outpatient.

B: Oh, that's OK. I see the sign now. I can get there all right, thanks! This hospital is so confusing.

A: That's the truth! I get lost here myself, and I work here!

INSIDE YOUR BODY (pp. 162-163)

Conversation 1: *What's happening?*

A: Oh, gee, look at this picture of the inside of a body!

B: Yeah. This guy's pretty colorful, isn't he? Red brain, green lungs.

A: Pink stomach, orange appendix, blue liver. Are livers blue?

B: A cow's liver in the supermarket is dark reddish-brown. But I've never seen a human liver. I have no idea what color it is!

A: I'm sure my heart is red. I've seen human hearts in medical shows on TV.

B: And I'm sure our bones are white. Skeletons always have white bones.

A: That's true. I wonder what all those other organs are.

B: Well, that purple thing behind the liver is the kidney, and the pink dot near the larynx is the tonsils. . .

Conversation 2: *What's the process?*

A: What about Number eight? When you have a stroke, what part of the body is affected?

B: Mmm. . . That's a hard one.

C: What's a stroke?

D: I don't know exactly what happens, but my grandmother had one, and it affected her whole body.

A: I think it's when there's a blood clot in your brain, and so the brain doesn't get oxygen.

B: Yeah. Lots of people die from strokes.

D: My grandmother was paralyzed and she couldn't talk.

C: How sad! That sounds terrible.

D: Oh, it was. But she recovered! She's fine now.

THE DENTIST (pp. 164-165)

Conversation 1: *What's next?*

A: I have to go to the dentist this afternoon. I'm so nervous.

B: Why? What's wrong?

A: Well, I'm just going to get my teeth cleaned. I don't think there's anything wrong, but you never know. . .

B: I know what you mean. I'm always afraid when I go to the dentist. I'm afraid he'll find some awful thing wrong.

A: Right, and he'll say, "Sorry, I have to pull all your teeth out."

B: Exactly. I have nightmares about going to the dentist.

A: I think a lot of people do. Poor dentists. Nobody wants to visit them!

B: Well, good luck this afternoon.

A: Thanks, I'll need it!

Conversation 2: *What's your opinion?*

A: Do you like your dentist, Don?

B: Yeah, he's good. And he's a pretty funny guy.

A: Funny?

B: Yeah, he tells jokes while he's working on you. There you are, lying in the chair with your mouth wide open. You can't say anything, and you can't laugh, but he's telling jokes.

A: Does he give a local anesthetic for fillings?

B: Yes, if you want it. I usually don't—I hate needles!

A: Well, I don't like needles, but I hate pain! The first thing I say when I sit down in that chair is "Give me something, anything—as long as I can't feel a thing!"

B: Not me. Of course, I've never had many cavities. I have pretty good teeth. I guess I'm lucky.

THE VETERINARIAN (pp. 166-167)

Conversation 1: *What's next?*

A: Do you have a pet, Sue?

B: Uh-huh. I have a cat. His name's George.

A: George, huh? That's a strange name for a cat, isn't it?

B: Really? Well, that's his name. He's a beautiful cat.

A: What does he look like?

B: He's black and white. He's very large, like a small dog, and his hair is long.

A: How old is he?

B: George is getting pretty old. He's sixteen now. Actually, I'm worried about him. He hasn't been eating well for about a week, and he doesn't seem to have any energy. He's just not himself.

A: Maybe you should take him to the vet.

B: I think you're right, Yumi. I'll call the vet after class.

Conversation 2: *What's happening?*

A: What's your dog's name? She's cute.

B: Her name is Munchi. She's so nervous that she's shivering. She always gets nervous when I bring her to the veterinarian.

C: My cat, Ernie, loves it here! They treat him so well! But he hates to be in this cage.

B: Well, I only bring Munchi here to board her. We board both dogs. That's ours, too—the big one. Her name is Tiny.

D: But Tiny loves it here—she's very friendly.

A: My dog, Chaco, here, never gets nervous. But I never board him. He's having a rabies inoculation today, but the injection doesn't bother him.

D: Injections never bother Tiny, either. She loves the vet, and she loves the assistant.

B: Munchi hates injections and she hates to be away from home. Maybe that's a difference between a large dog and a small one!

UNIT 10: LEISURE

LEISURE TIME (pp. 170-171)

Conversation 1: *What's the process?*

A: Do you ever watch TV, Kiki?

B: Yup. Every day. I love TV!

A: Hmm. . . I don't know what to check for your answer, Kiki. There's no place on this chart to check "every day."

B: What do you mean?

A: Look at the instructions. It says, "Check SOMETIMES or NEVER." "Every day" isn't "sometimes," and it isn't "never." So, what do I check?

B: Oh, I see what you mean, Ted. I don't know.

C: Check SOMETIMES.

A: But "Every day" isn't "sometimes."

C: That's true. But, Kiki watches TV sometimes every day. You don't watch TV all day, do you, Kiki?

B: No, of course not.

C: See? So it's "sometimes." Check SOMETIMES, Ted.

Conversation 2: *What's happening?*

A: What do you like to do most in your leisure time, Tony?

B: I like to work on my car. And I like to play with my pet snake, Slim.

A: Pet snake! Really? How do you play with a snake?

B: He likes to coil around me—it keeps him warm.

A: I don't think I'd like that, Tony. He could hurt you!

B: Oh, no, Slim never hurts me. He's a friendly snake. Sometimes we play hide-and-seek. He hides, and I seek. Sometimes I can't find him.

A: You can't find him? Oh, my. . . What do you do?

B: I put a mouse in his cage. He always comes back for dinner!

GOING OUT (pp. 172-173)

Conversation 1: *What's next?*

A: Do you go out a lot, Coco?

B: No, not much, Bob. I like to stay home. How about you?

A: Me? Yeah, I like to go out with my friends.

B: Out where?

A: Oh, just out. Anywhere. Sometimes we take in a movie. Sometimes just drive around. . . You stay home all the time?

B: Not all the time. I like to hang out with my friends. Usually we just hang out at my house.

A: Oh, yeah? What do you do?

B: Oh, listen to music, talk. . . You know, girl stuff.

A: Uh-huh. Well. . . I was wondering. . . Would you like to go out with me sometime, Coco?

Conversation 2: *What happened?*

A: OK, who likes to ride on a roller coaster?

B: I do.

C: Me, too.

A: What about you, Jen?

D: Well, it's not my favorite thing to do. It makes me dizzy.

C: Exactly! That's why it's fun!

D: Not for me. I went on a roller coaster one time, and that was enough for me!

B: Why? What happened?

D: I was so dizzy after the ride, I couldn't walk. I had to lie down on the ground right in the middle of the amusement park! Everybody was looking at me. It was so embarrassing! Never again!

A: Well, how about the Ferris wheel?

WATCHING TELEVISION (pp. 174-175)

Conversation 1: *What's next?*

A: Oh, I saw the best movie last night!
B: Yeah? What was it?
A: *Casablanca.*
B: That's a classic! Was it on TV?
A: No, I rented the video. It was so romantic!
B: Yeah, that's a great movie. I haven't seen it for years!
A: Do you ever watch videos, Bob?
B: Not very often. I don't have a VCR. And, you know, when I'm not studying, I'm usually out with my friends.
A: Of course. Well, you can come to my house to watch videos. It's a good way to study English. . .
B: I'd like that, Coco.

Conversation 2: *What's the process?*

A: Let's do this Community Activity together. OK, Van?
B: All right, Nicki. Do you have the TV schedule?
A: Right here. We have to choose one day. You pick the day.
B: Monday!
A: My, you said that pretty fast. Monday, huh? What's so special about TV on Monday?
B: "Monday Night Football"! Channel 4!
A: But I don't like American football, Van.
B: That's OK. You don't have to. But think about this— "Monday Night Football" takes the whole evening. If we write that, we're finished. Our work is done!
A: Hmm. . . that's an interesting thought. I think I do like "Monday Night Football," Van!

MOVIES (pp. 176-177)

Conversation 1: *What's next?*

A: Bob asked me to go to the movies tonight.
B: He did? All right! You really like Bob, don't you?
A: Well, I think he's very nice. We'll see. . .
B: What movie are you going to?
A: I forget the name. It's a mystery—with some romance, I think.
B: Sounds good. Who's in it?
A: One of my favorite actors, Harrison Ford.
B: Oh, I love Harrison Ford! His movies are great! Have a wonderful evening, Coco. And tell me all about it tomorrow!

Conversation 2: *What's the process?*

A: OK, guys. We have to write a role play. It says, "Include roles for everyone."
B: But we need at least five people to do this role play, and there are only four of us. Will one of us role-play two roles?
C: No, that's not what it means, Lei. See, it says, "Choose one of these situations." That means just the friends going to a movie. . .
D: Or just the woman selling tickets, or the usher collecting tickets. . .
B: But that's only one or two roles. It's still not the right number.
C: We have to make up the other roles.
B: You mean, like, maybe two friends waiting in line, talking to two other people in line?

C, D: That's it. That's the idea.
B: Or, maybe, two friends buying tickets and popcorn?
A: Exactly. Now we have to decide what they'll say.

INDIVIDUAL SPORTS (pp. 178-179)

Conversation 1: *What's your opinion?*

A: What do you think, Jim? Which individual sport is the most dangerous?
B: Oh, I don't know. Boxing, I guess. Remember that boxer that got killed?
C: But that doesn't happen very often. I think skiing is more dangerous. Lots of people break their legs skiing.
D: I think a lot of sports can be dangerous. People get hurt playing all kinds of sports.
A: That's true. People fall and die climbing mountains.
D: And people fall and get hurt riding bicycles, or skating, or snowboarding, or even jogging or playing tennis. . .
A: And some people drown when they're swimming.
B: True, but I still think boxing's the most dangerous. Boxers always get hurt!

Conversation 2: *What next?*

A: Do you do any individual sports, Stefan?
B: Well, I jog every day. And I go mountain biking or hiking with my girlfriend on weekends when the weather's good. That's about it. How about you, Ellen?
A: I love tennis. I play every time I can find a partner. Does anyone else play tennis?
B: I never got into tennis much, sorry.
A: Do you play tennis, Teresa?
C: Me? Oh, I'm not very athletic. I've tried a lot of sports, but I can't do anything very well.
A: How about you, Charlie?
D: Yep. Tennis is my game, too. But I don't know if you'd want to play with me. It can get pretty rough—I have a wicked serve!
A: Oh, yeah? Me, too!
B: I think you've found a new partner, Ellen.

TEAM SPORTS (pp. 180-181)

Conversation 1: *What's happening?*

A: What a great idea—going to a baseball game. I love baseball!
B: Some of us don't understand the game, though. I feel kind of silly here.
C: Baseball is very popular in my country. My father always took us to a game. I love baseball!
B: I'm glad I'm sitting next to you, then. Could you explain things to me?
C: Sure. OK, see the score? Our team is losing by one run.
D: And look who's coming to the plate—our best hitter!
(*Batter hits foul ball.*)
A, C, D: Watch out!
B: What's going on?
A: Look—a foul ball just landed at your feet! That's really lucky. . .

(Batter hits home run; crowd is cheering.)

B: What happened? Why is everyone going crazy? Oh, will I ever understand this game?

Conversation 2: *What's next?*

A: Did you watch the basketball game last night?

B: No. I wanted to, but I had to study. Who won?

A: Chicago. They were losing by one point with three seconds left in the game, and Jordan made two free throws to win the game!

B: Sounds like I missed a good game.

A: Yeah, Jordan had 45 points, and I don't think he missed a foul shot the whole game!

B: Wow! Hey, Ken, do you play basketball?

A: Yeah. Well, I played on my high-school team. Now I just shoot baskets when I have time. How about you?

B: I used to, but I haven't played in a while. Actually, I'd like to start playing again.

A: You know, there's a basketball court in the park near the school. How about shooting some hoops with me after class?

AT THE PARK (pp. 182-183)

Conversation 1: *What's happening?*

A: Grandpa, it's fun in the park!

B: I know, Danny. It's great to be here with you. Look at these pigeons! They're hungry.

A: Grandpa, why are the pigeons hungry?

B: Because it's lunch time, Danny. Don't throw that stone at the squirrel!

A: Why not, Grandpa?

B: Because you'll hurt him. You're a strong boy, Danny, and the squirrel is small.

A: What is that girl doing?

B: She's pushing a doll carriage, Dan. Looks like her brother is riding his bicycle.

A: Grandpa, what are those kids doing?

B: They're playing on the jungle gym and in the sandbox. Do you want to play with them, Danny?

A: No, Grandpa. I want to stay with you and ask more questions. I love you, Grandpa.

Conversation 2: *What's next?*

A: This lesson about parks reminds me of the parks back home. I'm getting homesick, I think.

B: What are the parks like? I'm from such a small town, there's only a plaza and a small park with some benches and flowers. It's pretty, but only interesting when there's a band playing.

C: Oh, the parks where I come from are very large and beautiful. The gardens are magnificent! They look different in every season. There are jogging paths, playgrounds for the children, and areas to play Frisbee, or ball, or even fly a kite.

D: That sounds like the park I remember so well—I feel so bad when I think of it. I went there when I was a little girl. There was even an amusement park inside the park.

A: What happened to it?

D: Oh, there was a terrible hurricane that destroyed the park. It's never been the same since then.

A, B: Oh, that's awful. How sad.

C: Carla, have you been to the park near the school? It's really beautiful.

D: No. I didn't even know there was a park.

C: How about going with me after class? I bet it will make you feel better.

D: Oh, that's so nice of you, Tom. Thanks!

TAKING A TRIP (pp. 184-185)

Conversation 1: *What's happening?*

A: Remember that contest I entered last semester? Well, guess what! I won! I won a cruise for two!

B: That's wonderful! Congratulations!

C: I'm so happy for you! Who is going with you?

A: My sister. We're going to Vancouver and Alaska in June on a cruise ship!

C: That's fabulous. What sightseeing will you do?

A: Well, we'll see the glaciers in Alaska and Mount McKinley in Denali Park. What else? Here's the travel brochure. Let's see. . . an abandoned gold mine, a reindeer farm, a boat ride up the Yukon. . . And so much in Vancouver, too. Let's see. . . Stanley Park, Granville Island. . . I'm so excited!

B: Do you need a passport to go to Canada?

A: I guess I should check to see if I need anything to get into Canada. I need to know how much luggage we can bring, too.

C: Well, don't forget your camera! We all want to see the photos!

Conversation 2: *What's next?*

A: What are you all doing for spring break?

B: My favorite thing—I'm going home. I go home for every vacation.

C: I'm going on a motorcycle trip to the desert with Carlos. We'll camp out at night and ride all day!

B: Riding through the desert can be hot this time of year. Be careful.

A: What are you going to do, Sonia?

D: I'm staying home. I wanted to go to the mountains; my cousins have a cabin there. But I really should look for a new job.

C: That's too bad. Well, good luck on your job search!

D: Thanks. Just remember me when you're all having a good time!

AT THE BEACH (p. 186)

Conversation: *What's your opinion?*

Teacher: A real treat for you all! We're going to the beach today!

Students: What? Terrific! Yea! Great!

Teacher: In our imaginations!

Students: Ah! That's no fun!

Teacher: Sh! Take your seats. . . Close your eyes. OK, everyone, take a deep breath. Visualize your favorite beach. Think about the sand and the surf; the blue sky and the sun. Is everyone at the beach now?

Students: Oh, yeah! Yes! Uh-hmm.

Teacher: Keep your eyes closed. What do you see?

A: I see a sailboat, and I'm the captain. It's a red sailboat. There's a nice breeze, and I'm moving along.

B: I see a surfboard, and I'm riding the waves. Oops, I just fell in the ocean!

C: And I'm on the lifeguard chair, watching her fall into the ocean. Can you swim?

D: I see my children playing with a pail and shovel, building a sand castle.

E: I'm sleeping in the sun on my beach towel. I've just put on suntan lotion.

Teacher: OK, everyone. Open your eyes. Tell me where you were?

CAMPING (p. 187)

Conversation: *What's next?*

A: This camping trip is great! It's so relaxing to be out here so far from the city!

B: I agree. This was a great idea! Nothing but earth and sky! Look at those stars!

C: This fire is difficult to start. Can anyone help me?

D: Oh, no! The wood is all wet! We'll never get a fire started!

A: Don't say that! Now that the sun is down, it's getting cold!

B: Well, let's turn in. No use freezing. . .

C: What was that noise?

A: Sounds like a bear!

D: There aren't any bears around here. But I wonder what it is. . .

THE LIBRARY (p. 188)

Conversation: *What's happening?*

A: Our term paper is due on Monday, Ralph. Let's stop fooling around and get some work done!

B: Don't worry, we'll get it done. We have two pages of notes already!

A: We need a six-page term paper! We have a long way to go!

B: No problem. We can use pictures. See, this encyclopedia has lots of good photographs we can copy.

A: We can't get away with that, Ralph. We have to *write* six pages!

C: Hi, Hiroko. Hi, Ralph. What are you two doing in the library? Finishing your term paper?

A: Oh, hi, Connie. Yeah. . . the reference librarian is getting some periodicals for us.

B: Yeah, yeah. We're just about finished. How about you?

C: Oh, we finished ours yesterday. I just hope it'll be OK.

A: I'm sure it will. Why are you worried?

C: Well, it's supposed to be six pages long, but ours is ten. We had so much information that we couldn't make it any shorter.

A, B: Oh. . .

SCHOOL (p. 189)

Conversation: *What's the process?*

A: Wow—last class! This semester went fast, didn't it?

B: Sure did! Just about the last page in the book, too. Let's please try to finish this Group Discussion.

A, C, D: OK. Yeah. Sure.

C: OK. I'll start. What other courses can you take where you study English? Oh, I guess that's here, huh?

D: Let's see. . . There are so many courses: math, computers, science.

A: Yes, and languages, history, anthropology. . . even photography and art!

C: OK, next question: Have you ever taken another course? Which one?

B: I took a secretarial course once. That was all.

A: And I took an auto mechanics course. The reading was too hard for me.

C: Question 3: Would you like to take another course? What course?

A, B, D: Of course! Yes! Engineering. Math. English. Ceramics. . .

C: Hold on! One at a time. Quick, let's finish. The bell is about to ring!

D: I'll do the last question: Do many adults go to school in your country? What kinds of courses can adults take?

A: Adult education is just really starting in my country. The government sponsors a lot of technical courses.

B: In my country, lots of adults take courses. Many adults study English, but they also study all different things.

C: In my. . .
(*Bell rings*.)

A, B, D: We did it! We finally finished an activity! Yea!

GRAMMAR FOR CONVERSATION CONTENTS

GRAMMAR FOR CONVERSATION

UNIT 1

VERB *TO BE*

Question

Where	am are is is are are are	I you he she we you they	from?

Affirmative

You're I'm He's She's You're We're They're	from Africa.

Negative

You're not I'm not He's not She's not You're not We're not They're not	from Asia.

PRESENT TENSE: REGULAR VERBS

Question

Where	do do does does do do do	I you he she we you they	live?

Affirmative

You I He She You We They	live live lives lives live live live	in San José.

Negative

You I He She You We They	don't don't doesn't doesn't don't don't don't	live	there.

PRESENT TENSE & SHORT ANSWERS

Question

Do Do Does Does Do Do Do	I you he she we you they	have	a pet?

Affirmative

Yes,	you I he she you we they	do. do. does. does. do. do. do.

Negative

No,	you I he she you we they	don't. don't. doesn't. doesn't. don't. don't. don't.

IMPERATIVES
Affirmative–Negative

Look!	Don't look.
Guess!	Don't guess.

Affirmative–Negative

Tell.	Don't tell.
Write.	Don't write.

DEMONSTRATIVE PRONOUNS: THIS/THAT/THESE/THOSE

This	is my photo.
That	is your photo.
These	are my sisters.
Those	are your parents.

THERE IS/THERE ARE

There is	one teacher.
There are	twenty students.

INTERROGATIVES
Question

What	is your name?
Who	is he?
Where	do you live?
How many	students are there?

Answer

My name is Sue.
He's my brother.
I live in Arizona.
There are 15 students.

PRESENT CONTINUOUS TENSE
Question

What	am are is is are are are	I you he she we you they	wearing?

Affirmative

You're I'm He's She's You're We're They're	wearing	sandals.

Negative

You're not I'm not He's not She's not You're not We're not They're not	wearing	boots.

220

POSSESSIVES

Possessive Adjective

My		
Your		
His		
Her		
Its	hair	is black.
The boy's		
Our		
Your		
Their		
The boys'		

Possessive Pronoun

Mine	
Yours	
His	
Hers	
Its	is black.
The boy's	
Ours	
Yours	
Theirs	
The boys'	

IRREGULAR NOUNS

Singular	Plural
1 child	2 children
1 man	2 men
1 woman	2 women
1 wife	2 wives

UNIT 2

ADJECTIVES

| He's | hungry.
thirsty.
sick.
happy.
tired. |

| He's a | hungry
thirsty
sick
happy
tired | man. |

ADVERBS & OTHER EXPRESSIONS OF FREQUENCY

| When
When
How
How
How | do you go to class?
does she study?
does he work?
does he eat?
does she read? |

| I go
She studies
He works
He eats
She reads | early.
late.
hard.
slowly.
fast. |

| How
What time
How often
What about
How about | are you?
do you get up?
do you watch TV?
Sally?
this? |

| I | always
usually
never | get up early. |

| I get up early | every day.
every morning.
sometimes. |

PHRASAL VERBS

Oh, hi! **Come in.**
I **get up** early.
I **get out of** bed right away.
I **get dressed** quickly.
He **gets ready** for work fast.
I **go to** bed late.
She **looks like** her sister.

They **punch in** at work.
They **punch out** after work.
Please, **sit down.**
Sit up, please.
Don't **stand up.**
He **wakes up** late.

DO/MAKE

do the dishes	make the bed
do the laundry	make coffee
do the shopping	make dinner
do homework	make friends
do housework	make my day

PREPOSITIONS

The students are **in** the classroom.
The clock is **on** the wall.
He's coming **into** the room.
Their feet are **under** the table.
She eats dinner **at** home.
She goes **to** school.
He gets **out of** bed.
He leaves **for** work.

SET PHRASES

Hey!
Oh, my!
You, too?

UNIT 3

PAST TENSE: *TO BE*

Question

Where	was were was was were were were	I you he she we you they	yesterday?

Affirmative

You I He She You We They	were was was was were were were	at home.

Negative

You I He She You We They	weren't wasn't wasn't wasn't weren't weren't weren't	at work.

PAST TENSE: REGULAR VERBS

Question

Where	did	I you he she we you they	live	last year?

Affirmative

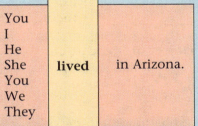

You I He She You We They	lived	in Arizona.

Negative

You I He She You We They	didn't	live	in New York.

PAST TENSE: IRREGULAR VERBS

Question

Where	**did**	I you he she we you they	**go**	last year?

Affirmative

You I He She You We They	**went**	to Canada.

Negative

You I He She You We They	**didn't**	**go**	to Hawaii.

IRREGULAR VERBS: PAST FORMS

blow/**blew**	have/**had**	teach/**taught**
come/**came**	make/**made**	think/**thought**
do/**did**	read/**read**	wear/**wore**
give/**gave**	say/**said**	write/**wrote**
go/**went**	see/**saw**	

OBJECT PRONOUNS

Direct Object

Niki	saw	me. you. him. her. it. us. them.

Indirect Object

John	gave	me you him her us them	a present.

Object of Preposition

Roberto went to the beach	**with**	me. you. him. her. it. us. them.

John gave a present	**to**	me. you. him. her. us. them.

MORE INTERROGATIVES

Whose **What kind of** **Which** **Why**	birthday is it? celebration is it? holiday is your favorite? do you like it?

UNIT 4

ADJECTIVES

Positive

The jar is	large. small. inexpensive. expensive. a good buy.

Comparative

This jar is	larger than smaller than less expensive than more expensive than a better buy than a worse buy than	the other one.

Superlative

This jar is	the largest the smallest the least inexpensive the most expensive the best buy the worst buy	of all.

PLURAL NOUNS

one tomato/two tomato**es**
one head of lettuce/two head**s** of lettuce
one box of cereal/two box**es** of cereal
one loaf of bread/two loa**ves** of bread
one dozen eggs/two dozen eggs

FUTURE: *WILL*

Question

What	will	I you he she we you they	bring?

Affirmative

You'll I'll He'll She'll You'll We'll They'll	bring	a fork.

Negative

You I He She You We They	won't	bring	a knife.

FUTURE: *GOING TO*

Question

What	am are is is are are are	I you he she we you they	going to	make?

Affirmative

You're I'm He's She's You're We're They're	going to	make a salad.

Negative

You're not I'm not He's not She's not You're not We're not They're not	going to	make a dessert.

CAN

Question

How	can	I you he she we you they	help?

Affirmative

You I He She You We They	can	wash	dishes later.

Negative

You I He She You We They	can't	help	now.

226

TAG QUESTIONS & ANSWERS

You	can eat will eat eat are eating ate	lunch,	can't you? won't you? don't you? aren't you? didn't you?	Yes, I can. Yes, I will. Yes, I do. Yes, I am. Yes, I did.
You	can't eat won't eat don't eat aren't eating didn't eat	lunch,	can you? will you? do you? are you? did you?	No, I can't. No, I won't. No, I don't. No, I'm not. No, I didn't.

POLITE EXPRESSIONS

May I help you?
Can I help you?
What would you like?
I'd like a hamburger, please.
Could I have mustard, please.
Would you prefer ketchup?
That'll be $2.00.
Have a nice day!   You, too!

SET PHRASES

By the way. . .
Here it is!
I can't wait!
Let see. . .

Lucky you!
That's too bad!
What a surprise!

Wish me luck!
You bet.
You name it!

MORE IRREGULAR VERBS: PAST FORMS

bring/**brought**
buy/**bought**
eat/**ate**
lose/**lost**
put/**put**

UNIT 5

PRESENT PERFECT TENSE: REGULAR VERBS

Question

How long	have have has has have have have	I you he she we you they	lived	there?

Affirmative

You've I've He's She's You've We've They've	lived	there since June.

Negative

You I He She You We They	haven't haven't hasn't hasn't haven't haven't haven't	lived	there very long.

FOR/SINCE

I've lived in Seoul	for	a little while. two years. a long time.

I've lived in Seoul	since	last November. 1985. I was four years old.

SHOULD

Question

What	should	I you he she we you they	do?

Affirmative

You I He She You We They	should	turn off	the water.

Negative

You I He She You We They	shouldn't	do	that!

228

SET PHRASES

Are you kidding?	Let me see. . .	What a day!
at all	Now, what?	Wow!
I guess so.	Oh, my goodness!	You guessed it!
I'm afraid so.	So did we.	

PHRASAL VERBS & IDIOMS

eat out	grab a bite to eat
fill in	keep an eye on
fool around	

PRESENT PERFECT TENSE: IRREGULAR VERBS

Question

How long	have have has has have have have	I you he she we you they	been	there?

Affirmative

You've I've He's She's You've We've They've	been	here a few minutes.

Negative

You I He She You We They	haven't haven't hasn't hasn't haven't haven't haven't	been	here very long.

IRREGULAR VERB FORMS

Simple	Past	Past Participle
be	was/were	been
bring	brought	brought
buy	bought	bought
choose	chose	chosen
cost	cost	cost
do	did	done
eat	ate	eaten
get	got	gotten/got
give	gave	given
go	went	gone
have	had	had
keep	kept	kept

Simple	Past	Past Participle
make	made	made
pay	paid	paid
put	put	put
read	read	read
ride	rode	ridden
see	saw	seen
sell	sold	sold
send	sent	sent
spend	spent	spent
take	took	taken
wear	wore	worn
write	wrote	written

PRESENT, PAST, FUTURE, & PRESENT PERFECT TENSES (REVIEW)

Question

Do	I/you/we/you/they	write?
Does	he/she/it	write?
Did	I/you/he/she/it/we/you/they	write?
Will	I/you/he/she/it/we/you/they	write?
Have	I/you/we/you/they	written?
Has	he/she/it	written?

Affirmative

Yes, you/I/you/we/they	write.
Yes, he/she/it	writes.
Yes, you/I/he/she/it/you/we/they	wrote.
Yes, you/I/he/she/it/you/we/they	will write.
Yes, you/I/you/we/they	have written.
Yes, he/she/it	has written.

Negative

No, you/I/you/we/they	don't write.
No, he/she/it	doesn't write.
No, you/I/he/she/it/you/we/they	didn't write.
No, you/I/he/she/it/you/we/they	won't write.
No, you/I/you/we/they	haven't written.
No, he/she/it	hasn't written.

COMPARISON OF TENSES

Present: I	go	to the store	every Friday.
Present Continuous: I	am going	to the store	now.
Past: I	went	to the store	yesterday.
Future: I	will go	to the store	tomorrow.
Present Perfect: I	have gone	to the store	many times.

MAY
Polite Offer/Permission/Possibility

May I help you?	Yes, thanks. I'd like to try on some shoes.
May I ask a question?	Yes, of course. What is it?
Where will you go shopping?	Well, I **may** go to the mall, but maybe not.
What will you buy?	I'm not sure. I **may** not buy anything.

EVER

Question

Do you	ever	shop	
Did you	ever	shop	
Will you	ever	shop	at a sale?
Can you	ever	shop	
Have you	ever	shopped	

Short Answers

Affirmative	Negative
Yes, I do.	No, I don't.
Yes, I did.	No, I didn't.
Yes, I will.	No, I won't.
Yes, I can.	No, I can't.
Yes, I have.	No, I haven't.

INTERROGATIVES

How	will you pay?
How many	hats do you have?
How much	does it cost?
How often	do you go shopping?
What	did you buy?
What kind	of flowers do you like?

When	do you buy medicine?
Where	do you like to shop?
Which	one do you prefer?
Who	can type?
Whose	calculator is this?
Why	did you buy it?

SET PHRASES

Aren't you lucky!	I know what	Pardon me.	That's so true.
Check out. . .	you mean.	Really?	To be honest. . .
Clear?	I'll take it!	Right!	Uh-oh!
Come on.	I'm sorry.	Take a look. . .	Wait a minute.
Don't worry.	I sure do.	Tell you what. . .	What's the matter?
Exactly.	I understand.	That's about it.	Why not?
Excuse me.	Let's go!	That's all.	Yes, of course.
Hey, good idea!	Like today.	That's OK.	You're kidding!
I bet. . .	Listen up.	That sounds good.	
I hope so.	Oh, no!	That's right.	

PHRASAL VERBS & IDIOMS

come over	keep up	Does that count?
get sick	made up (make up)	I'm all thumbs.
go around	sold out (sell out)	

232

UNIT 7

PRESENT, PAST, FUTURE, & PRESENT PERFECT TENSES: *TO BE* (REVIEW)

Question

Where	am are is was were will have has	I? you/we/you/they? he/she/it? I/he/she/it? you/we/you/they? I/you/he/she/it/we/you/they I/you/we/you/they he/she/it	be? been? been?

Affirmative

I'm You're/We're/You're/They're He's/She's/It's I/He/She/It **was** You/We/You/They **were** I/You/He/She/It/We/You/They **will be** I've/You've/We've/You've/They've **been** He/She/It **has been**	at school.

Negative

I'm **not** You're/We're/You're/They're **not** He's/She's/It's **not** I/He/She/It **wasn't** You/We/You/They **weren't** I/You/He/She/It/We/You/They **won't be** I/You/We/You/They **haven't been** He/She/It **hasn't been**	on the train.

COMPARISON OF TENSES: *TO BE*

Present:	I'm at the office **now**. I'm **usually** at work by 8:30.
Past:	She **was** at the bank **yesterday**.
Future:	We **will be** at the laundromat **tomorrow morning**.
Present Perfect:	I **have been** at the post office **many times**.

233

PRONOUNS: SUBJECT/POSSESSIVE/OBJECT (REVIEW)

Subject

I You He She We You They	went to the bank to cash

Possessive

my your his her our your their	check.

Direct Object

The police arrested	me. you. him. her. us. you. them.

Indirect Object

The clerk gave	me you him her us you them	a book of stamps.

Object of Preposition

Yoshi talked **to**	me you him her us you them	on the phone.

DIRECTIONS & LOCATION

Go straight.
Turn left at the corner.
The theater is just before the corner.
Ellis Island is close to the Statue of Liberty.
The number is next to the telephone.
It's in the trash near the building.

POLITE REQUESTS

Excuse me. How can I get to the post office?
Can you tell me how to get to the library?
Could you please tell me where I can park my car?
Pardon me. Do you know where I can make a phone call?
May I please speak to Richard?
May I take a message?
Please leave a message.

INTENSIFIERS

It's a **very** busy neighborhood.
There are **lots** of stores.
I **just** moved.
Just look at these dirty clothes!
The clothes **even** smell cleaner!
I'm **too** sick to go to the game.
How careless!

PHRASAL VERBS

Fill out this form.
Get on the train.
Get off at Copley Station.
I **grew up** in this neighborhood.
Someone **broke into** my car last night.
The police **took down** the information.
The thief **ran away.**
They **moved into** the house last Saturday.
We **looked for** the car.
We **rode around** the parking lot.
When Washo **came along,** my laundry got cleaner!

PREPOSITIONS

He lives **near** a playground.
The ambulance is **between** the hospital and the church.
The postal worker is **behind** the counter.
There are two mail boxes **in front of** the post office.
A firefighter is **on top of** the building.
Nosey's News is **next to** Nick's Market.
The police station is **across from** the bank.
There's a flag **outside** the high school.
Turn just **before** the Food Mart.
The bank is just **after** City Hall.

SET PHRASES

Freeze!
Got it?
Guess what!
Here it is.
Here you are.
I'm telling you. . .
It goes. . .
No problem.
No way!
right away
Take care!
the right of way
Too bad. . .

UNIT 8

HAVE TO

Question

Do you have to wear	a uniform?
Does he have to work	all night?
Do they have to help	with the housework?

Affirmative

Yes, I do. I have to wear	a uniform.
Yes, he does. He has to work	all night.
Yes, they do. They have to help	with the housework.

Negative

No, I don't. I don't have to wear	a uniform.
No, he doesn't. He doesn't have to work	all night.
No, they don't. They don't have to help	with the housework.

SOME/ANY/NONE/EVERY

Question	Affirmative	Negative
Are there **any** signs?	Yes, there are **some** signs.	No, there are **no** signs.
	Yes, there are **many** signs.	No, there are**n't any** signs.
Is **anyone** hurt?	Yes, **someone** is hurt.	No, **no one** is hurt.
	Yes, **everyone** is hurt.	No, **nobody** is hurt.
Is **anybody** working?	Yes, **somebody** is working.	No, **nobody** is working.
	Yes, **everybody** is working.	No, **none** of them are working.
Did he do **anything**?	Yes, he did **something**.	No, he did**n't** do **anything**.
	Yes, he did **everything**.	No, he did **nothing**.
Did you go **anywhere**?	Yes, we went **somewhere**.	No, we did**n't** go **anywhere**.
	Yes, we went **everywhere**.	No, we went **nowhere**.

NONE OF US ➝ ALL OF US

None of us have jobs.
A few of us have jobs, but **most of us** don't.
Not many of us have jobs; **most of us** don't.
Some of us have jobs, and **others** don't.
Many of us have jobs, but **some** don't.
Most of us have jobs, but **a few** don't.
All of us have jobs.

SET PHRASES

apply in person	Danger: High Voltage!	No Admittance
Authorized Personnel Only	Do Not Touch!	No problem.
Be careful.	Emergency Exit Only	pay attention
call in sick	get fired	sick of. . .
Caution!	Good luck on the job!	Thanks for seeing me.
check it out	It's against the rules.	want ads
city slicker	Keep Out!	Wear your hard hat!
collect unemployment	keep track of	work experience

UNIT 9

ADJECTIVES & ADVERBS

Positive

> ### Adjectives
> I'm **sick**.
> We're **healthy**.
> This meal is **nutritious**.
>
> ### Adverbs
> You need to act **quickly** in an emergency!
> I **often** have headaches.

Comparative

> ### Adjectives
> She's **sicker**.
> You're **healthier**.
> This meal is **more nutritious than** that one.
>
> ### Adverbs
> You need to act **more quickly**.
> He has headaches **more often than** I do.

Superlative

> ### Adjectives
> He's the **sickest**.
> They're the **healthiest**.
> This is the **most nutritious** meal of all.
>
> ### Adverbs
> EMTs act the **most quickly**.
> She has headaches the **most often**.

GOOD–BAD

Positive

> This is **good** medicine.
>
> She has a **bad** toothache.

Comparative

> This medicine is **better than** that medicine.
> His toothache is **worse**.

Superlative

> This is the **best** medicine of all.
>
> My toothache is the **worst**.

REFLEXIVE PRONOUNS

I		myself.
You		yourself.
He		himself.
She	hurt	herself.
It		itself.
We		ourselves.
You		yourselves.
They		themselves.

SET PHRASES

Better than ever!	main entrance
family practice	medical problem
general practice	not so good
Get well soon!	operating room
health center	Ouch!
HIV test	patient information form
How do you feel?	so-so
How sad!	Stand back!
I feel better.	That sounds terrible.
I feel fine.	waiting room
internal medicine	well baby clinic

UNIT 10

MODALS & SIMILAR EXPRESSIONS

Ability
Can you play basketball?
We **could** come later.

Advice
We really **should** get more exercise.
You **ought to** take another course.

Invitation/Offer
Will you play on my team?
Would you like to go to the movies?

Possibility (Maybe)
I **may** take a trip next spring.
I **might** go to Peru.

Probability (Probably)
He **must** be very tired—he's sleeping through the game!
You **would** like that movie, I'm sure!

Necessity
I **have to** be home by midnight.
We **must** finish this report by 5:00!

Recommendation/Suggestion
You **should** hear Suzie sing! She's wonderful!
We **could** go to Le Club. . .

DO LIKE/WOULD LIKE

What **do** you **like** to do?

What **would** you **like** to do?

I **like** to play baseball, travel, and read.
I **enjoy** playing baseball, traveling, and reading.

I**'d like** to go to the beach.
I **want** to go to the beach.

STORY SEQUENCE CONNECTORS

First of all, I made a reservation.
Then I bought my ticket.
After that, I made a list of things to take.
Next, I went shopping for casual clothes.
Later, I packed my suitcase.
Finally [At last, In the end], I said goodbye to my family and left on my trip.

PHRASAL VERBS & IDIOMS

My favorite TV show **comes on** at eight o'clock.
It's fun to **drive around**.
We can't **get away with** that!
I **get homesick** when I travel.
Don't **get sunburned**!
He likes to **go camping**.
Baseball games sometimes **go on** for hours.
I like to **go out** with my friends.
My sister and I **hang out** together.
I want to **lie down** and take a nap.
Did you ever **ride on** a Ferris wheel?
Let's **turn in**—it's getting late.
Watch out for the bears!

SET PHRASES

Hold on!
I'm so happy for you!
I see what you mean.
That's wonderful!
We did it!
What's going on?

AFRICA

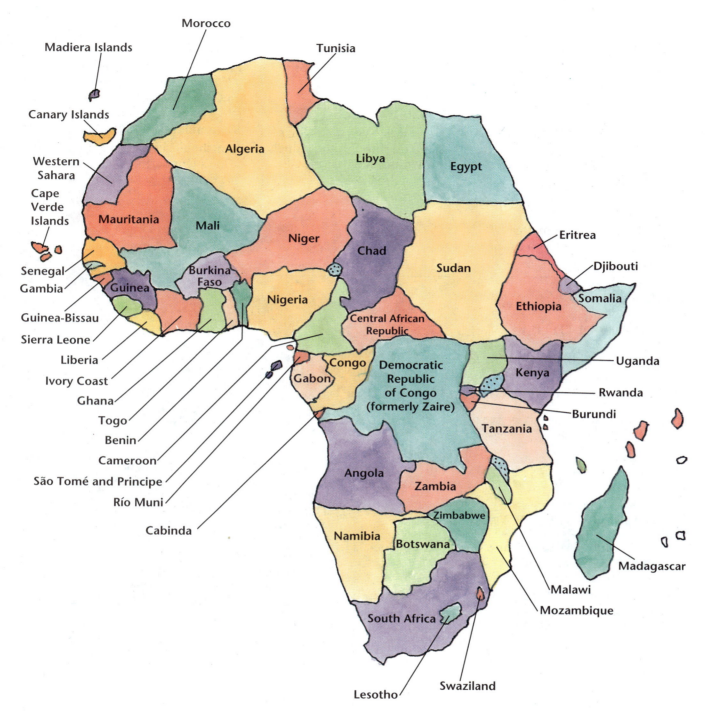

Madiera Islands

Canary Islands

Western Sahara

Cape Verde Islands

Senegal

Gambia

Guinea-Bissau

Sierra Leone

Liberia

Ivory Coast

Ghana

Togo

Benin

Cameroon

São Tomé and Principe

Río Muni

Cabinda

Morocco

Tunisia

Algeria

Libya

Egypt

Mauritania

Mali

Niger

Chad

Sudan

Eritrea

Djibouti

Somalia

Ethiopia

Burkina Faso

Nigeria

Central African Republic

Guinea

Congo

Gabon

Democratic Republic of Congo (formerly Zaire)

Uganda

Kenya

Rwanda

Burundi

Tanzania

Angola

Zambia

Zimbabwe

Malawi

Mozambique

Madagascar

Namibia

Botswana

South Africa

Lesotho

Swaziland

ASIA AND AUSTRALIA

Turkey
Kuwait
Lebanon
Syria
Cyprus
Afghanistan
Israel
Iraq
Iran
Jordan
Saudi Arabia
Yemen
Oman
United Arab Emirates

Bhutan
Nepal
Pakistan
Mongolia
China
India
Hainan Island
Bangladesh
Myanmar (Burma)
Thailand
Sumatra
Malaysia
Singapore
Java
Borneo
Brunei
Cambodia
Vietnam
Laos

N. Korea
S. Korea
Japan
Taiwan
Hong Kong
Philippines
Indonesia
Papua New Guinea

Australia
Tasmania
New Zealand

EUROPE

Iceland

Northern
Ireland   Scotland
Republic of   Sweden
Ireland   Norway   Finland

Denmark   Estonia
Wales   Latvia   Lithuania
Netherlands   Russia
England
Belgium   Germany   Poland   Belarus   Ukraine
Luxembourg
France   Czech Republic
                               Slovakia   Azerbaijan
                    Austria   Hungary
Spain   Switzerland   Italy   Romania   Moldova
Portugal   Corsica Slovenia   Bulgaria   Turkey   Georgia
          Sardinia   Croatia   Yugoslavia Armenia
                                                                Macedonia
          Sicily   Albania   Greece
              Bosnia and
              Herzegovina

Greenland (Denmark)

Iceland

Alaska (U.S.)

Canada

United States of America

Hawaiian Islands (U.S.)

Mexico

Bahamas

Cuba

Haiti

Dominican Republic

Puerto Rico

Belize

Honduras

Guatemala

El Salvador

Nicaragua

Costa Rica

Panama

Ecuador

Guyana

Suriname

French Guiana

Venezuela

Colombia

Peru

Brazil

Bolivia

Argentina

Paraguay

Chile

Uruguay

UNITED STATES OF AMERICA (U.S.A.) AND CANADA

NATIONS/NATIONALITIES

Notice that many nationalities end in *-ese, -ian, -ish, -an*, or *-i*.

NATION	NATIONALITY	NATION	NATIONALITY
	(-ese)		**(-an)**
China	Chinese	Chile	Chilean
Japan	Japanese	Costa Rica	Costa Rican
Lebanon	Lebanese	Cuba	Cuban
Portugal	Portuguese	The Dominican Republic	Dominican
Senegal	Senegalese		
Sudan	Sudanese	Kenya	Kenyan
Taiwan	Taiwanese	Korea	Korean
Vietnam	Vietnamese	Mexico	Mexican
		Puerto Rico	Puerto Rican
	(-ian)	South Africa	South African
Argentina	Argentinian	Uganda	Ugandan
Australia	Australian	United States of America	American
Brazil	Brazilian		
Canada	Canadian	Venezuela	Venezuelan
Egypt	Egyptian		
Ethiopia	Ethiopian		**(-i)**
Haiti	Haitian	Israel	Israeli
Hungary	Hungarian	Kuwait	Kuwaiti
India	Indian	Pakistan	Pakistani
Indonesia	Indonesian	Saudi Arabia	Saudi
Iran	Iranian	Somalia	Somali
Italy	Italian		
Lithuania	Lithuanian		**(irregular)**
Nigeria	Nigerian	France	French
Panama	Panamanian	Germany	German
Peru	Peruvian	Greece	Greek
Romania	Romanian	Netherlands	Dutch
Russia	Russian	Switzerland	Swiss
		Thailand	Thai
	(-ish)		
Denmark	Danish		
England	English		
Ireland	Irish		
Poland	Polish		
Spain	Spanish		
Sweden	Swedish		
Turkey	Turkish		

NAMES/NICKNAMES

Notice that some men's and women's nicknames are the same or have the same pronunciation. Many nicknames for children end in -y. Some names do not have nicknames. Add more names to the list.

MEN

GIVEN NAME	NICKNAMES
Albert	Al, Bert
Alexander	Alex, Al
Alfred	Al, Fred
Andrew	Andy, Drew
Anthony	Tony
Arnold	Arnie
Brian	_____
Christopher	Chris
Daniel	Dan, Danny
David	Dave, Davey
Edward	Ed, Eddie, Ted, Teddy
Eugene	Gene
Francis	Frank, Frankie
Gerald	Gerry, Jerry
James	Jim, Jimmy
Jason	Jay
Jeffrey	Jeff
John	Jack, Johnny
Joseph	Joe, Joey
Joshua	Josh
Justin	_____
Lawrence	Larry
Lee	_____
Louis	Lou, Louie
Mark	_____
Martin	Marty
Matthew	Matt, Matty
Melvin	Mel
Michael	Mike, Mikey
Nathaniel	Nat
Nicholas	Nick, Nicky
Patrick	Pat
Paul	_____
Peter	Pete, Petey
Richard	Dick, Rich, Rick, Ricky
Robert	Bob, Bobby, Rob, Robbie
Scott	Scotty
Sean, Shawn	_____
Stephen, Steven	Steve, Stevie
Terence	Terry
Theodore	Ted, Teddy
Thomas	Tom, Tommy
William	Bill, Will, Billy, Willy

WOMEN

GIVEN NAME	NICKNAMES
Abigail	Abby
Alison, Allison	_____
Andrea	Andy, Andi
Ann, Anne	Annie
Ashley	_____
Barbara	Barb, Barbie
Carol, Carole	_____
Carolyn	_____
Catherine	Cathy
Christine	Christie, Tina, Chrissy, Chris
Cynthia	Cindy
Dorothy	Dot, Dottie
Elaine	_____
Elizabeth	Beth, Betsy, Betty, Liz
Emily	Em, Emmy
Faith	_____
Fay, Faye	_____
Frances	Fran
Gail	_____
Gloria	_____
Heather	_____
Helen	_____
Hope	_____
Jacqueline	Jackie
Jane	_____
Janet	Jan
Janice	_____
Jean, Jeanne	Jeannie
Jeanette	_____
Jessica	Jess, Jessie
Joan	Joannie
Joanne	Jo
Judith	Judy
Kathleen	Kathy
Laura	_____
Laurie	_____
Linda	_____
Lisa	_____
Margaret	Peggy, Peg, Maggie
Martha	Marty
Mary	_____
Maryanne	_____
Nicole	Niki
Patricia	Pat, Patty, Patsy
Rebecca	Becky
Roberta	Bobbie
Rose	Rosie
Sally	Sal
Sandra	Sandy
Sharon	Sherry
Stephanie	Steph
Susan	Sue, Susie
Teresa, Theresa	Terry, Terri

GOSSIP SECRETS

UNIT 5, PAGE 63: *City or Country*

I was born and grew up on a farm in the country. It was very peaceful and beautiful. Then I went to the city with my husband. I did not like the city. It was too noisy and crowded. Now my family and I live in a town in the mountains. We are happy there.

UNIT 5, PAGE 71: *The Living Room*

I love my living room. I stay in the living room all day. Sometimes I lie on the sofa and watch TV. Sometimes I listen to music and sleep in the armchair. Sometimes I walk on the coffee table and eat the plant there. I like to play with the pillow on the sofa and the lampshade on the lamp. I am a beautiful yellow cat.

UNIT 9, PAGE 162: *Inside Your Body*

Last week, a nineteen-year-old girl came to the hospital with her aunt. The girl was very weak and very tired. Her blood tests showed a problem, but she did not want treatment. Her religion was against medical treatment. The girl's aunt was angry. She said, "You must have treatment!" The girl said, "No. God will give me treatment." Then she and her aunt went away. They did not come back, so we don't know what happened.

UNIT 10, PAGE 189: *School*

In January, I started a computer course at a community college. The first class was very difficult. After class, my car didn't start. It was snowing and cold. I was very unhappy. Fortunately, a student from my class helped me with my car. He helped me with the computer course, too. We studied together all semester. I got an "A" in the course, and next week we are getting married! What a wonderful semester!

UNIT 9: REVIEW

(PAGE 168)

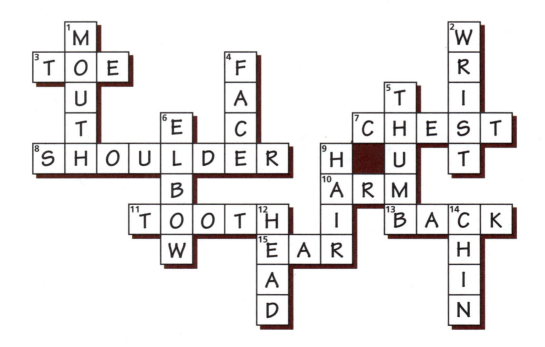

SPEECH EVALUATION FORM

Speaker's Name: _____

Date: _____

Speech Topic: _____

	Needs Work	Satisfactory
Organization	_____	_____
Pronunciation	_____	_____
Vocabulary	_____	_____
Eye Contact	_____	_____
Visual Aids	_____	_____

Best Part of Speech: _____

Recommendations: _____

Evaluator's Name: _____

AUDIENCE EVALUATION FORM

Speaker's Name: _____

Date: _____

Speech Topic: _____

	Needs Work	Satisfactory
Attentiveness	_____	_____
Quietness	_____	_____
Eye Contact	_____	_____
Appropriateness of Questions	_____	_____
Form of Questions	_____	_____
Number of Questions	_____	_____
Responsiveness	_____	_____

Recommendations: _____

_____

Evaluator's Name: _____

NOTE: Make as many copies of these forms as you need.

THE HUMAN BODY

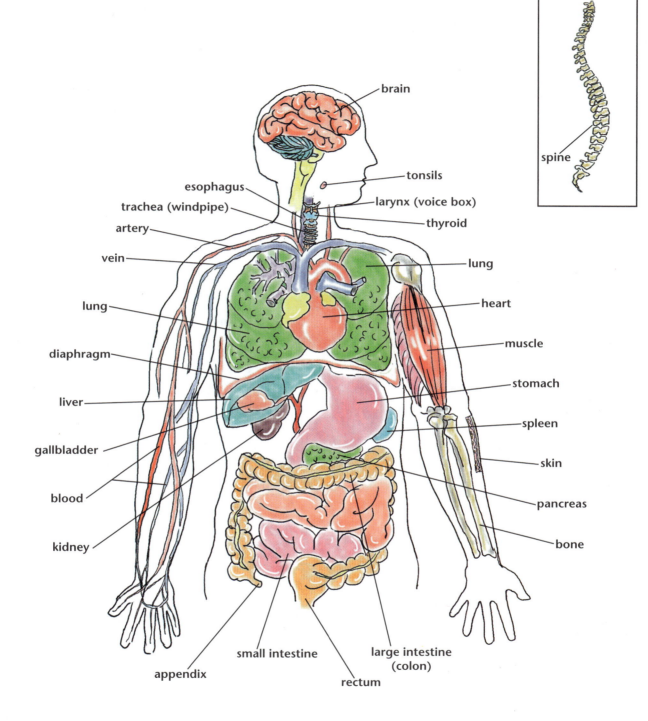

brain

spine

esophagus

trachea (windpipe)

artery

vein

lung

diaphragm

liver

gallbladder

blood

kidney

tonsils

larynx (voice box)

thyroid

lung

heart

muscle

stomach

spleen

skin

pancreas

bone

small intestine

appendix

large intestine (colon)

rectum

ALPHABETICAL WORD LIST TO PICTURE DICTIONARY

A

abscess, 164
accelerator, 122
accident, 158
account (bank), 118
    (savings), 118
ache, 154
across from, 108
activity, 33
activity (physical), 178
actor, 176
actress, 176
adding machine, 101
address, 111
admit, 176
ADMITTING (sign), 161
adult, 10
adult ed, 189
advantages, 121
advertisements, 102
advice, 153
aerobics, 178
Africa, 4
afternoon, 18
ago, 26
aide (hospital), 132
    (teacher), 132
AIDS test, 152
ailment(s), 154
air, 124
air mail, 116
airplane, 184
airplane ticket, 184
aisle (supermarket), 58
aisle (theater), 176
a la mode, 48
alarm clock, 18
allergy (allergies), 154
allergy & immunology, 156
always, 51
a.m., 18
ambulance, 112
amusement park, 172
anesthetic, 164
angry, 17
animal, 48
ankle, 150
answering machine, 110
antacid, 96
antenna, 174
apartment (building), 106
apartment (flat), 64
appendicitis, 163
appendix, 162
apple, 42
apple pie, 33
appliances, 92
    (small), 66
appropriate behavior, 140
apricot, 42
April, 28
apron, 134
argue, 16
arm, 150
armchair, 70
around the corner, 108
arrest, 114

artery, 162
artichoke, 44
ash tray, 57
Asia, 4
aspirin, 74
assembly line, 136
assistant, 166
astronaut, 134
athletic (equipment), 84
Atlantic Ocean, 4
ATM (automated teller
    machine), 118
attendant, 124
at the beach, 186
attic, 64
audience, 176
audiocassette(s), 101
audiovisual, 188
August, 28
aunt, 10
author, 188
AUTHORIZED PERSONNEL
    ONLY (sign), 137
automated teller machine
    (ATM), 118
automatic (shift), 122
autumn (fall), 34
awning, 64
ax, 112

B

baby, 20
baby seat, 122
baby shoes, 88
baby-sit, 76
back, 150
backache, 154
backpack, 187
bacon, 50
badge, 134
bag (feed), 139
    (golf), 84
    (mail), 116
    (shopping), 91
bagel, 50
baggage (luggage), 184
baggie (plastic), 52
bake, 47
balcony, 64
bald, 2
ball (bowling), 84
    (golf), 84
    (soccer), 84
ballet dancer, 134
balloon(s), 30
banana, 42
band, 32
bandaid(s), 74
bank, 108
bankbook, 118
bank officer, 118
bank training, 144
bar (candy), 56
    (chocolate), 56
    (salad), 54
barbecue, 47
barber, 132

barn, 138
barnyard, 138
barrette, 8
baseball, 84
    (base), 180
    (bat), 84
    (cap), 84
    (catch), 180
    (game), 170
    (glove), 84
    (hit), 180
    (out), 180
    (pitch), 180
    (run), 180
    (umpire), 180
basement, 64
basil, 47
basket (laundry), 125
    (picnic), 182
basketball, 84
    (basket), 180
    (dribble), 180
    (foul), 180
    (free throw),
180
    (hoop), 180
    (pass), 180
    (shoot), 180
bat, 84
bathing suit, 39
bathrobe, 90
bathroom, 74
bath towel(s), 74
bath toy(s), 74
bathtub, 74
battery (batteries), 130
beach, 34
beach blanket, 186
beach chair, 186
beach towel, 34
beach umbrella, 186
bean, 44
bear, 187
beard, 2
beautiful, 62
bed, 18
bedroom, 72
bedspread, 72
beef (ground), 46
    (roast), 46
    (stew), 46
beer, 57
bee sting, 159
beet, 44
behavior, 140
behind, 108
belt, 8
bench, 36
benefits, 146
best wishes (ribbon), 94
between, 108
beverage, 48
bicycle, 86
bicycling, 178
bikini, 39
bill (amount), 71
bin (recycling), 106
binder (3 ring), 100

bird, 34
Birth Center, 156
birthday(s), 30
birthday cake, 30
birthday card(s), 100
black, 2
black & white TV, 101
blackberry, 42
blanket, 72
bleach, 125
block(s) (street), 108
blond, 2
blood, 162
blood pressure, 152
blood test, 152
blood transfusion, 160
blouse, 8
blow out (the candles), 30
blue, 2
blueberry, 42
boar, 138
board (chalkboard), 14
board (wood), 130
board game(s), 86
body (inside), 162
    (parts), 150
boil, 47
boiled ham, 52
bologna, 52
bolt(s), 99
bone, 162
book, 14
    (read), 70
bookcase, 70
book of stamps, 116
boombox (portable stereo
    system), 101
boots, 9
    (Western), 88
    (winter), 88
    (work), 88
borrow, 76
boss, 140
bother, 76
bottle, 58
bottle return, 58
bouquet, 94
bowl (cereal), 50
    (salad), 68
    (soup), 68
    (sugar), 66
bowling, 178
bowling ball, 84
box, 42
    (lunch), 52
    (tool), 99
boxer shorts, 9
boxing, 178
box spring, 72
boy, 2
bra (brassiere), 91
bracelet, 98
braces, 164
brain, 162
brake, 122
brand, 97
brand name, 59
bread, 52

cry, 16
cucumber, 44
cup(s), 30
cupboard, 66
curly, 2
curtains, 72
    (shower), 74
custodian, 134
customer, 54
customer service, 92
cut flowers, 94
cutoffs, 39
cycle(s) (laundry), 125

D

daffodil, 94
daisy, 94
damaged goods, 102
dance, 172
danger, 114
DANGER: HIGH VOLTAGE
  (sign), 137
Danish, 50
dark wash, 125
darts, 86
date(s), 28
daughter, 10
day, 20
day after tomorrow, 26
day before yesterday, 26
December, 28
Declaration of
  Independence, 32
decorating (cake), 189
decorations, 32
deduct, 146
deer, 187
defrost the freezer, 128
delivery, 116
dental hygienist, 164
dental receptionist, 144
dentist, 164
dentist's chair, 164
deodorant, 74
department, 82
department store, 82
deposit box, 118
deposit slip, 118
dermatology, 156
desert, 62
desk, 14
    (courtesy), 58
desk calendar, 100
dessert(s), 48
detergent, 125
diamond, 98
diapers, 96
diaphragm, 162
dictionary, 188
different, 21
digital clock, 18
dill, 47
dining room, 68
dinner, 18
director of public relations,
  144
directory assistance, 110
dirty, 125
disability, 146
discount place, 103
discrimination, 140
dish(es), 20
    (soap), 74
dishpan, 66
dishwasher, 66

distance (long), 110
district manager, 141
divorced, 2
dizzy, 154
do(es) (homework), 20
    (housework), 128
    (laundry), 20
doctor, 156
dog, 10
dog collar, 166
dog groomer, 144
dog tag, 166
doll, 86
doll carriage, 182
domestics, 92
dominoes, 170
DO NOT ENTER (sign), 123
DO NOT TALK TO
  OPERATOR, 136
DO NOT TOUCH (sign),
  137
door, 14
    (front), 120
    (rear), 120
doorknob, 14
dormitory, 64
doughnut, 48
dozen, 58
drain, 74
drama, 174
drapes, 70
draw, 16
drawer, 72
dress, 8
dressed, 22
dresser, 72
dressing room, 93
dress shirt, 90
dress(ed) up, 172
dribble (basketball), 180
drink(s) (beverage)(s), 56
    (coffee), 22
    (soft), 54
drip, 78
drive-in/drive thru window,
  54
driver, 120
drown, 186
dry, 38
dry-clean, 125
dry cleaner, 125
dryer, 66
dry the dishes, 128
duck (toy), 86
duck, 138
duckling, 138
due, 188
duplicate (key), 99
dust storm, 36
dust the furniture, 128

E

ear (of corn), 44
ear, 150
earache, 154
early, 18
earmuffs, 39
earrings, 2
east, 38
eat (breakfast), 18
    (dinner), 18
    (lunch), 18
egg, 34
    (fried), 50

eight, 6
eighteen, 6
eighteenth (18th), 28
eighth (8th), 28
eighty, 6
EKG (electrocardiogram),
  158
EKG LABORATORY EXAM
  ROOM (sign), 161
elbow, 150
electrical tape, 99
electric drill, 99
electric mixer, 66
electric razor, 74
electric train(s), 86
electrocardiogram (EKG),
  158
electronic equipment, 101
electronics, 92
electronics store, 82
elevator, 92
eleven, 6
eleventh (11th), 28
emerald, 98
emergency (fire), 112
    (medical), 158
    (police), 114
EMERGENCY (sign), 161
emergency brake, 122
EMERGENCY EXIT ONLY
  (sign), 137
Emergency Medical
  Technician (EMT), 112
emergency room, 158
employee, 140
employer, 140
employment application,
  145
encyclopedia, 188
end of season (sales), 102
engagement ring, 98
engine (automobile), 124
    (fire), 86
engineer (construction),
  132
    (railroad), 120
enter, 120
entrance, 120
entree, 52
envelope(s), 100
equipment, 134
    (athletic), 84
    (electronic),
    101
erase, 16
eraser, 14
escalator, 92
esophagus, 162
espresso, 48
Europe, 4
evening, 18
every day, 26
everyday, 20
everyday life, 13
ewe, 138
exact change, 120
examination table, 166
exciting, 62
excuse, 140
excuse me, 19
exercise, 150
exhaust pipe, 122
exit, 120
expensive, 88
exterminator, 78
extraction (tooth), 164

extra large (XL) (size), 90
eye(s), 2
eye examination, 152

F

face, 150
factory worker, 132
faint, 158
fall (autumn), 34
fall, 158
family, 10
family care, 156
family leave, 146
family practice 156
fare, 120
farm, 62
farm market, 44
farm stand, 34
farm worker, 132
fast, 121
fast food, 54
father, 10
father-in-law, 10
faucet, 66
favorite, 11
fax machine, 101
February, 28
feed bag, 139
feed(s) (the baby), 20
    (the birds), 182
    (the dog), 128
feet, 31
fence, 64
fender, 122
fern, 94
fever, 154
field, 139
field goal (football), 180
fifteen, 6
fifteenth (15th), 28
fifth (5th), 28
fifty, 6
fight, 76
file cabinet, 100
filling (tooth), 164
film, 96
final sale, 102
find(ing) a job, 144
fine, 188
finger, 150
fingernail, 150
fins (swim), 184
fire, 112
fire (dismiss from job), 142
fire engine, 86
fire escape, 112
fire fighter, 112
fire hydrant, 112
fireplace, 70
fire sale, 103
fireworks, 32
first (1st), 28
first class (mail), 116
first level (parking), 92
fish, 46
fisherman, 132
fishing, 84
fishing reel, 84
fishing rod, 84
fit (clothing), 88
five, 6
flag, 32
flame, 112
flashlight, 130
flat (apartment), 64